ZENDAYA IS LIFE

A Superfan's Guide to
All Things We Love about Zendaya

KATHLEEN PERRICONE

ILLUSTRATED BY KELLY SMITH

CONTENTS

INTRODUCTION

One of the most influential people on the planet, Zendaya Maree Stoermer Coleman is an actress, singer, dancer, fashionista, role model, creative force, and a cultural icon in the making. But, first, she was a Disney Channel teen superstar, starting on *Shake It Up* with Bella Thorne and then her own sitcom, *K.C. Undercover*. Zendaya's path from the House of Mouse to Hollywood was paved with selective film and television roles that highlighted her depth as an actress: a trapeze artist in 2017's *The Greatest Showman*, Peter Parker's love interest in Marvel's *Spider-Man* trilogy, and a high schooler struggling with drug addiction on the HBO series *Euphoria*. Before long, the Kids' Choice and Teen Choice Awards on her mantel were replaced by not one, but two Primetime Emmys—making her the youngest recipient in history for Outstanding Lead Actress in a Drama Series. Zendaya has done it all in style, literally. With the expertise of her "image architect," Law Roach, the actress topped every best-dressed list in the past decade (ever since she snuck onto the red carpet at the 2015 Academy Awards in vintage Vivienne Westwood). At her own film premieres, Zendaya embraces "method dressing"—she channeled a science fiction (sci-fi) robot in London for *Dune: Part Two*, while tennis was the theme of her *Challengers* promotional tour wardrobe in 2024. "Fashion is something I've always used as an outlet, a tool," Zendaya explained to the BBC. "Ultimately, I think I am a more shy person so it allows for me to create this persona, this character that I get to live in for the day."

She is not shy, however, when it comes to speaking her mind. Ever since her teens, Zendaya has often been the voice of reason, calling out everything from racism and sexism to unrealistic beauty standards. As a brand ambassador, she seeks out partnerships that strive for inclusivity and diversity. Authenticity, it seems, is her unique superpower in an industry that struggles with superficiality. Zendaya credits her Oakland, California, roots—as well as her parents and five older siblings—with always keeping her firmly grounded. "I'm really lucky to have the parents that I have," she gushed on *The Ellen DeGeneres Show*. "They just have always instilled in me those core values that I think I have to carry with me through everything."

For all her achievements, it is hard to believe Zendaya is not even thirty yet, even for those who know her best. "To me, Zendaya is a thousand years old," *Dune* franchise director Denis Villeneuve marveled to *Time*. "She has already lived many lives before this one.

"Ultimately, I think I am a more shy person so it allows for me to create this persona, this character that I get to live in for the day."

And, yet, she is as young as springtime. By some inextricable paradox, she also gives the impression of having been born sometime far into the future. She is timeless, and she can do it all . . . She seems fearless, her roots run deep, and I love that she still laughs like a kid. Zendaya is the future. And there is nothing more comforting to me." *Dune* costar Timothée Chalamet calls her "good-energy Hollywood," and someone who he often looks to while navigating their industry. "Just how much she's able to achieve while also sort of letting everything roll off her back is *mega*-inspiring," he told *GQ*. "She's just doing."

PART ONE

The "It" Girl

GOLDEN
CHILD

The baby of the family, Zendaya is more of an old soul—or "Grandma," as she is affectionately nicknamed. The precocious girl is wise beyond her years: She got straight A's, loves William Shakespeare, and used to spend her afternoons reading to the students in her mother Claire Stoermer's inner-city classroom in Oakland, California. Her peaceful disposition reflects her name, a twist on *tendai*, "to give thanks" in the Shona language spoken in Zimbabwe (her paternal ancestry traces back to Africa).

"I knew I wanted to be an entertainer. I could see myself singing and dancing in front of millions of people."

"My dad had a thing for Z's and zen," she told *Popstar! Magazine*, and thus, Zendaya was born on September 1, 1996.

Inside the Coleman home in Oakland's diverse Emeryville neighborhood, she was a vivacious spirit, adored by her five older siblings from her father Kazembe Ajamu's previous marriage. However, at school, the painfully shy kindergartner barely uttered a word. "Whenever I didn't understand something in class, I wouldn't raise my hand and say, 'Hey, I need help,'" Zendaya revealed on *Jimmy Kimmel Live*. "And they would just move on, and I couldn't keep up." At the end of the school year, Zendaya's parents decided to have the five-year-old repeat kindergarten, as they sought professional help on how to boost their daughter's confidence.

One suggestion was to put her in sports, so they enrolled Zendaya in a local basketball team. "I was supposed to be the first girl in the NBA, that was my dad's dream," she joked on Yahoo!'s *Daily Shot* in 2013.

"That died quickly." After one season of hooping, she lost interest and moved on to soccer and track, neither of which made an impression. "Then, I discovered dance!" Zendaya wrote in her 2013 tween self-help book, *Between U and Me*. At the age of eight, she joined hip-hop troupe Future Shock Oakland and found her groove popping and locking with kids twice her age. "I knew I wanted to be an entertainer. I could see myself singing and dancing in front of millions of people."

Her first role, however, was nonspeaking—and nonstanding. Zendaya, or "Z," as her friends call her, was cast as a silkworm in a school production of *James and the Giant Peach*, "which means that I literally laid on the stage and did absolutely nothing," she recalled to *Elle* in 2023. "I was incredibly shy, so I'm proud of myself for even trying to audition." Her interest in acting was officially piqued, and Zendaya had a front row seat to the magic at the California Shakespeare Theater (known as Cal Shakes), where her mother worked every summer as the house manager. She begged to tag along for nightly technical rehearsals, where it was the little girl's job to hold a flashlight on the director's script in the darkened amphitheater.

By the following summer, she graduated to passing out programs and selling raffle tickets to the audience and, if she was quiet, hanging out backstage with the actors. Once the performance started, "She had this routine," Claire recalled to the *San Francisco Chronicle*. "She would go to catering. They would give her a burrito and a Snapple. She would go up into the back of the house, grab a chair and a bunch of blankets, and just sit up in the back and watch the show." In third grade, Zendaya began taking theater classes at Cal Shakes, learning scenes from *Macbeth*, *As You Like It*, and *Richard III*. "I remember seeing her up there on that stage," said

Claire, "and just the few little moments that she had her spotlight, it was like, 'whoa.'"

Zendaya had a similar effect on Robert Kelley, artistic director of TheatreWorks in Palo Alto, California, when the eleven-year-old auditioned for the musical *Caroline, or Change* in 2008. "I just looked up, and there was the most striking human being I had ever seen in my whole life," Kelley told the *San Francisco Chronicle*. It was Zendaya's first professional theater gig—and she played a little boy in a short wig and denim overalls. For her next role, Little Ti Moune in *Once on This Island*, Zendaya was the only child in the production at Berkeley Playhouse; yet, she held her own with actors three times her age (and expertise), remembered producer Kimberly Dooley. "It's about a presence, an ability to look in your eyes and listen and be reflective and take notes and incorporate them and perform those notes, which can be really hard for kids. So, I was impressed right away that she could do that. There's something like a steadiness in her—a strong, calm center that she had even as a kid," said Dooley.

Offstage, Zendaya got to show her playful side as a fashion model for Old Navy, Macy's, and Mervyn's in and around the San Francisco area. But brighter lights were beckoning. Her agent suggested the twelve-year-old try her hand at auditioning in Los Angeles (LA). And, in early 2009, Zendaya and her father, Kazembe, made weekly six-hour treks from the Bay Area down the coast—and immediately she booked a Kidz Bop music video for a cover of Katy Perry's "Hot n Cold." At the shoot, Zendaya watched as the other young dancers flaunted their moves, "crazy stuff" to her like flips she had only attempted in her living room, but never successfully pulled off. It did not matter. "I was like, 'I'm not gonna be shown up, today,'"

"I just looked up, and there was the most striking human being I had ever seen in my whole life."

she reminisced on LA's REAL 92.3. When it was her turn, "little Zendaya decides out of nowhere that I'm going to try to do the flip . . . I did it, and I landed on my feet. I have never in my life done a front handspring." Her father was just as shocked. "Where did that come from?" Kazembe asked her. "Honestly Dad, I have no idea."

For her next gig, Zendaya shared the screen with someone she grew up watching on the Disney Channel, *Wizards of Waverly Place* star Selena Gomez. She was hired to be a background dancer in a Sears commercial, a minor role; yet, Zendaya "acted like a diva" on the set, she recalled eight years later to *Vogue*. That attitude did not fly with her father, who had quit his job to help his daughter find success in Hollywood. "We're going home," he warned her. "Dad, I can't go home a failure! I can't *not* do this," she begged him. Kazembe let her stay, and it was Zendaya's intensity in that moment that convinced him "she's goin' all the way."

DISNEY DARLING

Zendaya was one of two hundred girls who auditioned for Disney Channel's *Shake It Up*, a sitcom about teenage best friends who get their big break on the local dance show *Shake It Up Chicago*. She stood out to Judy Taylor, the vice president of casting and talent relations at Disney. "She's someone who walks into a room and makes you do a double take," the Disney executive told the *East Bay Times* in 2010. "You never tire of watching her."

Thirteen-year-old Zendaya originally tried out for the part of Cecilia "CeCe" Jones, the troublemaking half of the duo. During callbacks, producers asked her to also read for book-smart Raquel "Rocky" Blue and paired her with four other young actresses to test their chemistry, including actress Bella Thorne. Zendaya had previously crossed paths with the redhead at a print ad audition "and she literally twirled into the room," Zendaya recalled in *Between U and Me*. "I'd never seen someone do this before, and I was like, 'Who is this girl? Where is she coming from?'" Months later, at the *Shake It Up* audition, it clicked when she recognized Thorne. "I was like, 'Oh, yeah! The Twirl Girl!'"

The two instantly got along, and their chemistry was undeniable to Disney producers who cast Zendaya as Rocky opposite Thorne's CeCe in the teen buddy comedy. When she learned the good news, "I actually could not speak. I couldn't talk," Zendaya recalled to the BBC. "My dad looked at me like I was crazy, but I literally had nothing to say. That was one of those little speechless moments. I heard it and my mind went blank." On the set of *Shake It Up*, that summer, Zendaya eased into her very first acting gig like a seasoned pro, infusing part of her own personality into Rocky, such as the fact that she is a vegetarian and an animal lover. When the show premiered in November 2010, the pilot episode drew 6.2 million viewers, surpassing *Hannah Montana* as the highest-rated premiere in Disney Channel history.

Overnight, Zendaya was everywhere: on red carpets, at *Shake It Up* meet and greets on the cover of *Tiger Beat* magazine, and promoting her own Rocky-inspired clothing line at Target. She was even at the 32nd Annual World of Wheels car expo in Wichita Falls, Texas, where she signed autographs for fans. The popular teen was pulled in so many new and exciting directions that it was impossible for her to attend school like a regular kid—so, school came to her and the rest of the young cast on the Disney set. In between rehearsals and filming, Zendaya and Thorne spent five hours a day with their shared tutor studying history, biology, algebra, English, and Spanish. There were essays, tests, and plenty of homework that she had to complete before she was allowed to pick up a script and memorize her lines. If she did not maintain satisfactory grades, she could not be on the show. "So, that's a lot of pressure," Zendaya admitted in *Between U and Me*. "I'll graduate when I'm eighteen, just like any high-school kid—and I really want to go to college. I do miss the social aspect of being in a regular school, but I love the individual attention I get from my teacher. I don't have to raise my hand, but it's also hard to pass a note to Bella and not get caught!"

During Season 2 of *Shake It Up*, the costars portrayed a different set of best friends forever (BFFs) for the Disney Channel made-for-TV movie *Frenemies*: Halley (Zendaya) and Avalon (Bella Thorne) are editors of their own web magazine who battle to score an interview with the same pop star. Later that year, Zendaya became one herself when she signed a deal with Hollywood Records. In between studio sessions, she shot the third and final season of *Shake It Up* and competed on *Dancing with the Stars*, making it all the way to the finale with partner Valentin Chmerkovskiy, yet ultimately lost to *American Idol* contestant Kellie Pickler and Derek Hough. During the whirlwind, the sixteen-year-old was still expected to keep up with her grades (a tutor accompanied her on the road). "In the car. On the plane. On the train. In the hotel room," Zendaya recounted to *Glamour* all the places she snuck in studying. "[My teacher] would be like, 'Are you tired? I don't care.' I remember doing *Dancing with the Stars* and literally falling asleep reading a book. I'd never been so tired in my life—there's no off time."

"I think it's always important for kids to see themselves reflected on the screen, and when you're making child programming, you have a little bit of an extra responsibility there."

The same month *Shake It Up* aired its final episode in 2013, Disney announced Zendaya would star in her own sitcom, *Super Awesome Katy*, about the adventures of a teenage spy. One of the most in-demand young talents on the network, Zendaya leveraged her star power—she insisted that Disney let her be a producer on the show. In that role, her first move was to change the name of her character. "Do I look like a Katy to you?" she joked to *Vogue*. Instead, she became K.C., short for Katrina Charlotte Coretta Scott Cooper (her middle name pays homage to civil rights leader Coretta Scott King, the late wife of Martin Luther King Jr.). The lead character of *K.C. Undercover* is a brainiac with a black belt in martial arts and no singing or dancing talent whatsoever. "I didn't want them to all of a sudden be like, 'Oh, yeah, and then she sings this episode!' No. She can't dance; she can't sing. She can't do that stuff. There are other things that a girl can be."

Zendaya's other nonnegotiable: The show had to feature a Black family. "I just thought that that was important from the Disney Channel, considering that I know I watched it as a kid, and what I connected to the most was *That's So Raven*," she recalled to *The Hollywood Reporter* in 2021. "I think it's always important for kids to see themselves reflected on the screen, and when you're making child programming, you have a little bit of an extra responsibility there." Ratings proved that Zendaya had plenty of star power to carry her own show; the January 18, 2015, premiere of *K.C. Undercover* was the night's No. 1 children and family series on social media, according to Nielsen, a global leader in audience insights, data, and analytics.

Zendaya grew up along with her fanbase, and as she branched out into music, film, and fashion during breaks from the show, she experienced an overwhelming amount of support. "Replay," the lead single on her 2015 debut album *Zendaya*, was certified platinum with one million copies sold. Ahead of Season 2 of *K.C. Undercover*, she was cast in Marvel Studios' *Spider-Man* reboot, starring newbie Tom Holland and the Marvel Cinematic Universe (MCU)'s OG Robert Downey Jr., who reprised his role as Iron Man. In late 2016, she launched her clothing line Daya by Zendaya with pop-up shops in New York, Chicago, and LA—all of which she attended on the same day. "It's crazy," she gushed to the *LA Times*, as hundreds of people lined up down the block. "I thought nobody was going to come."

But, would they still be there if she was not a Disney star? Ahead of the third season of *K.C. Undercover*, Zendaya dropped hints it would be the last, as her character prepared to go off to college. She, too, was hoping to enter a new chapter, Zendaya confessed to *Entertainment Tonight* at *Variety*'s 2017 Power of Young Hollywood event. "I'm growing up, and there's a lot of other things I want to do in my career."

FASHIONABLE
APPROACH

The leap from Disney to Hollywood would not be child's play, but Zendaya had a secret weapon: her stylist Law Roach. The two first met in 2011, when the fourteen-year-old needed something to wear for her first major red-carpet event, the premiere of Justin Bieber's concert film, *Never Say Never*. Law Roach, who was working with Celine Dion at the time, dressed the *Shake It Up* starlet in a silver metallic blazer and light gray lacquered miniskirt that was youthful yet edgy. Three years later, as she was preparing to take the next step as the lead of her own show *K.C. Undercover*, Zendaya attended her first

New York Fashion Week, arriving each day in a different chic style. However, it was a yellow-and-blue full-length Miuniku coat that landed her on the cover of *Women's Wear Daily* the next morning—"and started all the frenzy," according to Law Roach. "She got out the car. Nobody knew who she was," he revealed to *The Verge* in 2018. "[But then] we started walking up the steps of Lincoln Center, and it was like one photographer, and then it was three photographers, and then it was six, and then it was twelve. It was crazy."

Until then, he had struggled to find designers who wanted to dress "the Disney girl," he recalled to *The Zoe Report* in 2019, "so I came up with this plan of attack for her . . . I spent a lot of time to build this blueprint for how I thought I could garner her acceptance in fashion." Calling himself an "image architect," Law Roach got creative constructing his teenage style muse, thoughtfully mapping out not only what she wore, but also where she wore it. He did not shy away from a fashion faux pas. "I would only put her in clothes that other people had worn because I knew, at that time, [magazine features on] people who had worn all the weekly styles were really popular," he told *TZR*. "So, I would only put her in things that people had worn, so that the designers would start to notice her and notice her name, and it actually worked out."

Zendaya had her own tricks up her fashionable sleeves. The actress did not have credentials to attend the 2015 Academy Awards, but that did not deter her. "Listen, I had no business being there," she admitted to *Access Hollywood* in 2021. "I was with an agent. They had an extra ticket, and I got to go, and I kind of snuck a little bit onto that red carpet." The eighteen-year-old, looking ethereal in an ivory Vivienne Westwood gown, had stayed up the night before getting her hair twisted into faux locs—and she simply could not pass up the opportunity to have it captured by cameras at the Hollywood event.

That year was also her first time at the Met Gala—and it was a legendary debut. For the night's theme, "China: Through the Looking Glass," Fausto Puglisi custom-made a dress with an embroidered miniskirt and train so voluminous that Zendaya actually had to travel to the event standing in a truck.

Her second Met Gala appearance was just as showstopping. For the 2016 event's theme, "Manus x Machina: Fashion in an Age of Technology," Law Roach dressed Zendaya in a form-fitting gold-sequined Michael Kors gown that took a month to embroider. The next year, Zendaya topped *Vanity Fair's* best-dressed list in a flowing Dolce & Gabbana gown adorned with tropical parrots for the theme "Rei Kawakubo/Comme des Garçons: Art of the In-Between." However, the highest compliment came from Rihanna, who was so wowed by Zendaya's Met Gala moment that she posted a photo of the Disney actress with the caption "brown goddess." The twenty-year-old hopped on Snapchat to properly freak out over the A-list approval. "Guys, I'm going through it right now. I never knew a post could mean so much to me, in all my life. That post alone, my skin is clearing up," she joked.

In 2017, as *K.C. Undercover* was coming to an end after three seasons, Zendaya the film star emerged from the Disney cocoon, literally. At the Australian premiere of *The Greatest Showman*—a musical based on P. T. Barnum in which she plays a trapeze artist—Law Roach dressed Zendaya in a Moschino butterfly gown that remains "one of my all-time favorites," Zendaya told *Vogue* in 2024. Explaining Law Roach's flair for "method dressing," Zendaya told the magazine: "With Law and I, we always find inspiration from films that I'm doing . . . [the butterflies] is this idea of being costumey. 'You're the greatest showman, everything is drama,' so that's what this dress was to me. It's like being literal, being dramatic, being entertaining. Also, that day, there was tons of butterflies. I went onto the carpet and there was butterflies everywhere, and I was like, 'It's a sign!'"

EVERYTHING
TO PROVE

When Zendaya imagined the next chapter of her acting career after *K.C. Undercover*, she saw the bigger picture: the movie world. Film offers rolled in; however, none felt quite right. "Having a Disney past sometimes makes it difficult for people to take you seriously," she confessed to *Glamour*, "so I have to pick the right projects, make sure I do the right things, take my time." As Zendaya explained to *Variety*, "I would much rather have one line in a great movie than be the lead of a shitty one." She actually had about ten lines in the $880 million

"I have to pick the right projects, make sure I do the right things, take my time."

Spider-Man: Homecoming as MJ, Peter Parker's sarcastic Academic Decathlon teammate and—spoiler alert!—eventual love interest.

The little screen time made a big impact on the audience and critics: "She brims with enough potential to make Marvel's next *Spider-Man* standalone into the most exciting title on their slate," praised *Indie Wire's* David Ehrlich. During the audition process, however, Zendaya was not so confident she would get the part, even though she aced her table read with Holland, who had already been cast as Peter. "A lot of time, the thought process of an actor of color is 'I'm going to go and give it my best shot, but they are probably not going to go with an actor of color for this,'" Zendaya revealed to *Variety*. "We all think it. I didn't know they were going to switch up the characters and really cast the best people for the roles, instead of what's most like the comic book. I think that was the coolest part for me, knowing they embraced the diversity."

She had also embraced Holland when they first met—just as he was going in for a handshake. "He says it was super awkward," Zendaya joked to *Variety*. "But I don't remember that. I thought it was cool." On the big screen, their chemistry was so convincing, fans wondered if it was more than just good acting skills. "We are friends," Zendaya insisted to the magazine. "He's a great dude. He's literally one of my best friends. This past how many months we've had to do press tours together. There's very few people that will understand what that's like at twenty years old." The two bonded over their experiences as child actors—Holland starred in *Billy Elliot: The Musical* in London for two years before transitioning from stage to screen in 2012's *The Impossible* opposite Naomi Watts. As the star of *Spider-Man*, "his life is about to change dramatically," Zendaya predicted to *Glamour*, "more than my life is about to change because I've already been in the public eye. For me, will it be heightened? Yes, but it's not anything that I wouldn't expect or have seen before." Her spidey sense must have been tingling because 2017's *Spider-Man: Homecoming* catapulted Holland to superstardom, particularly on Instagram, where his following doubled from 1.9 million to 5 million by the end of the year.

Zendaya's popularity also reached new heights, literally, in her next role: Anne Wheeler, a trapeze artist in *The Greatest Showman*, a musical loosely based on the life of P. T. Barnum, starring Hugh Jackman, Zac Efron, and Michelle Williams. The actress, who also got to showcase her singing talent in the film, flew right into acrobatic bootcamp before the start of production. "She was really hardcore," director Michael Gracey told *USA Today*. "She would send me photos of blisters all over her hands, and I would get videos of her flipping through the air and being caught. She went all in."

Although she was signed on for the second installment of the *Spider-Man* trilogy, 2019's *Spider-Man: No Way Home*, Zendaya still worried about the trajectory of her career. The anxiety over selecting her next role—and potentially making a wrong move—was so overwhelming, she admitted it was almost to the point of paralysis. "But I also wanted to prove myself," she confessed to *The Hollywood Reporter*. So, when the opportunity knocked to play a teen struggling with drug addiction on HBO's *Euphoria*, "I was very grateful because all those fears melted away and I felt like it was something that I had to be a part of. So, the fear became just, like, push yourself. If you go to work and you're scared, that's a good thing. You *should* be worried about whether you can do it."

Zendaya was also concerned about how her fans would react to the show's dark subject matter. Although she was twenty-two when *Euphoria* premiered in June 2019, many of her followers are years younger, so, before the first episode, she issued a warning about the mature content:"I have a heavy responsibility on my shoulders," she acknowledged to *The Hollywood Reporter*. "I just wanted to make sure that my fans knew, even the ones who were my age or older than me, that I still felt their support, even if they felt that the material was too triggering for them or if they didn't feel ready or comfortable watching. [At the same time,] I didn't want to limit [myself] as an artist. I want to be able to do the things that I want to do and play the roles that I want to play."

Zendaya's haunting performance as Rue Bennett was critically-acclaimed—and, in 2020, it earned her a Primetime Emmy Award for Outstanding Lead Actress in a Drama Series, beating out veterans Laura Linney (*Ozark*), Olivia Colman (*The Crown*), Jodie Comer (*Killing Eve*), Sandra Oh (*Killing Eve*), and Jennifer Aniston (*The Morning Show*).

"I would much rather have one line in a great movie than be the lead of a shitty one."

At home with her family due to the coronavirus, Zendaya accepted the award in her living room dressed in a custom Armani Privé bedazzled bralette and polka-dot skirt. Zendaya, the youngest to win the award and only the second-ever Black actress, took a moment to thank *Euphoria* creator Sam Levinson, whose own drug addiction inspired Zendaya's character, Rue. "I'm so grateful for you. I'm so grateful that you trust me with your story, and I hope I continue to make you proud."

LEADING LADY

Until she was twenty-four, the only characters Zendaya played were high schoolers—"and, mind you, I never went to high school," she joked to *Vogue*. In the 2021 romantic-drama *Malcolm & Marie*, the actress finally got to play a more age-appropriate character, the girlfriend of a writer-director (played by John David Washington) whose relationship is on the brink of collapse. Zendaya produced the black-and-white film, which was written and directed by *Euphoria* creator Sam Levinson and filmed during the COVID-19 lockdowns. She was eager to make a movie, albeit safely and adhering to protocols, before starting production on her third and final *Spider-Man* flick, *Spider-Man: No Way Home*, and knew Levinson had the talent to whip up a compelling story. "I was pitching Z horror films and psychological thrillers and all that, and then, at some point, I thought, well, what if it's just a relationship piece that plays out in real time," he recalled to *Deadline*.

Levinson was just as thoughtful when selecting the Malcolm to Zendaya's Marie. In John David Washington, the son of Denzel Washington, he found a "heavyweight" actor who could go toe-to-toe with the young star in the dialogue-heavy scenes, as the two argue over Malcolm not thanking his girlfriend at his film's premiere. Critics hyper-fixated on John David Washington being twelve years older than Zendaya, but Zendaya insisted it was merely the public's perception that she was so young. "People often forget—which is understandable because I've been playing sixteen since I was sixteen, you know—[but] I am grown," she told *People*. "I knew that, as I grow and as I evolve, there would be that moment where I could play someone my own age." On the set, Zendaya was the more senior of the two compared to John David Washington, a rookie actor with only a few credits to his name, including Christopher Nolan's *Tenet*. "I was leaning on her for a lot," he told *Variety*.

Zendaya appreciated Levinson creating a complex character like Marie, a former drug addict who's insecure in her relationship, that allowed her to showcase her range "as the woman he's grown to know, in front of his eyes," she explained to *Deadline*. "Sam writes female characters that are so layered and flawed and conflicted, but have such depth to them. I might say, well, I would never do that, I would never say that, or go there, but that's the point of doing it. I'm existing through this character."

"I knew that, as I grow and as I evolve, there would be that moment where I could play someone my own age."

While the pandemic accelerated the release of one film, another was delayed a year. *Dune: Part One*, the epic sci-fi adventure based on Frank Herbert's 1965 novel, features an ensemble cast rounded out by Timothée Chalamet, Rebecca Ferguson, Oscar Isaac, and John Brolin. Zendaya plays Chani, a warrior who appears to Paul (Chalamet) in his dreams before the two meet and fall in love—sharing their first kiss in *Dune: Part Two*, which grossed over $700 million worldwide. Zendaya and Chalamet only worked together for a few days on the first film and did not really get to know each other until the press tour, "so, when it came time to work together, it felt like we already had that shorthand," he told CNN in 2024. "I'm proudest of the love story in this movie, not in the moments where they're affectionate or in love, but in everything else that's earned. When you see relationships with young people in a lot of movies, it's usually that goo-goo gaga thing.

"I love being on set because it is not just creatively stimulating, but it's one of the few places where I feel free."

My favorite scene is when Paul's waking up from a nightmare and Chani is comforting him. They're very adult expressions of love."

Zendaya went from an ensemble cast to the marquee name for *Challengers*, costarring Josh O'Connor from *The Crown* and Broadway's Mike Faist. The actress also produced the tennis-themed drama centered around a toxic love triangle—and she worried about dropping the ball. "This is my first time leading a film in this way, so, ya girl's [sic] been nervous, but everyone's [sic] excitement and encouragement has meant the world to me," she captioned an Instagram post giving fans a behind-the-scenes peek at the production.

Zendaya was also concerned about the misperception of her "unlikable" character Tashi Duncan, an injured tennis ace who pits her husband (Faist) and ex-boyfriend (O'Connor) against each other, both personally and professionally on the court. "My job was trying to find her gooey center, her empathy, why she makes her decisions, and what pain it's coming from," she explained at a press conference in Sydney. "I think it's grief of a career and a life she never got to live. Her one true love was always tennis, and she is trying whatever she can to be close to it."

After playing a teenage spy, trapeze artist, Spider-Man's girlfriend, and a warrior on a desert planet, Zendaya wanted to "tap into the evil, supervillain vibes," she revealed to *Elle*. More so, it is her dream to one day direct a movie. But, first, she has to overcome the fear. "I love being on set because it is not just creatively stimulating, but it's one of the few places where I feel free," she confessed to *The New York Times* in a 2024 discussion about being "overly conscious of everything" in her life. "But I'm not at the place where I'm quite confident enough to step into directing." Working with the likes of the *Dune* franchise's Denis Villeneuve and Academy Award-nominated Luca Guadagnino, "I'm like, 'Let me sponge and get as much from this as possible' . . . So, hopefully, one day that confidence will kick in, but until then, I'll just keep learning."

PART TWO

New Hollywood

FILMOGRAPHY

Zendaya's IMDb page is the definition of diverse, with films and TV shows spanning comedy, drama, romance, action, science fiction, and musical. After getting her start on the Disney Channel as a teenager in Hollywood, the actress narrowed her focus to roles that showcased her true talents, ranging from a drug addict struggling to stay clean (HBO's *Euphoria*) to a rebellious warrior who must choose between love and loyalty (*Dune* franchise). Most impressively, Zendaya is critically acclaimed—two Primetime Emmys, a Golden Globe, seven Teen Choice Awards— and a commercial powerhouse with more than $5 billion at the global box office.

SHAKE IT UP

INTRODUCING DISNEY'S NEWEST STAR
PREMIERE DATE: NOVEMBER 7, 2010

The teen sitcom follows the adventures of BFFs Rocky Blue (Zendaya) and CeCe Jones (Bella Thorne), backup dancers on the popular local show *Shake It Up Chicago*.

CREATOR: Chris Thompson

CAST: Bella Thorne, Davis Cleveland, Roshon Fegan, Adam Irigoyen, Kenton Duty, and Caroline Sunshine

NETWORK: Disney Channel

SEASONS: Three

NUMBER OF EPISODES: Seventy-five

OPENING THEME SONG: "Shake It Up" by Selena Gomez

AWARDS: NAACP Image Award: Outstanding Performance in a Youth/Children's Program (nomination)

TWO TO TANGO: Zendaya and Thorne star as the overachieving Rocky and ditzy CeCe, respectively, "one of the most likable and engaging BFF duos we've ever seen," raved Gary Marsh, president of Disney

Entertainment. The cast is rounded out by the duo's friends: Rocky's brother Ty (Fegan), his pal Deuce (Irigoyen), CeCe's brother Flynn (Cleveland), as well as *Shake It Up Chicago* costars Gunther (Duty) and Tinka (Sunshine).

A buddy comedy for younger audiences, *Shake It Up* was created by Chris Thompson, a veteran TV producer who had previously worked on *Laverne & Shirley* and *Bosom Buddies*, the short-lived NBC sitcom best known for launching the career of Tom Hanks.

DANCE CRAZE: Capitalizing on the popularity of competition series *Dancing with the Stars* and *So You Think You Can Dance*, *Shake It Up*—television's first dance-driven sitcom—featured a variety of styles including contemporary, funk, jazz, hip-hop, tap, and even hula, which Zendaya practiced as a child for two years at the Academy of Hawaiian Arts in Oakland, California. Thorne, on the other hand, had no formal training and took dance classes three times a week to pull off the complicated choreography.

GOOD INFLUENCE: Zendaya related "a hundred percent" to Rocky, someone she described as a loving, caring "goody-two-shoes" who wore her heart on her sleeve. "Her main goal in life is to help people and dance," the fourteen-year-old told Radio Disney on the set of *Shake It Up* in 2010. But she also learned from the character's mistakes. "She gets into some sticky situations. Sometimes she gets uncomfortable about herself and then she wants to change, because she thinks she's too smart. It's all about being comfortable with yourself, so that's what I've learned from her."

SONG & DANCE: The original music featured on the series was compiled into three best-selling soundtracks. The first, *Shake It Up: Break It Down*, topped the *Billboard* Kid Albums chart in 2011 thanks to "Watch Me," a duet by Zendaya and Thorne, and the show's theme song, recorded by Selena Gomez, the star of Disney Channel's *The Wizards of Waverly Place*. The two-disc collection included an instructional DVD of dance steps and sold 500,000 copies, twice as much as 2012's *Shake It Up: Live 2 Dance*, which features the Zendaya pop solo "Something to Dance For." The third soundtrack, *Shake It Up: I Love Dance*, is more hip-hop influenced, like the kids chart-topping duet "Contagious Love."

KISS OFF: In Season 3, Rocky develops a crush on Logan Hunter (Leo Howard), a boy her age who nearly becomes CeCe's stepbrother until her mother Georgia decides not to marry Logan's father, Jeremy Hunter. But, when Zendaya read the script for the episode "Clean It Up" and saw it called for Rocky to kiss Logan, the fifteen-year-old refused. "I'm not gonna do this," she recalled thinking in a 2021 interview with British *Vogue*. "I'm going to kiss him on the cheek because I haven't been kissed, yet, so I don't want the kiss to be on camera." And that is as far as the romance went—after Logan refuses to get along with CeCe, Rocky dumps him.

FORMER FRENEMIES: In 2015, two years after *Shake It Up* had gone off the air, Thorne revealed that she and Zendaya were not originally friends. The first season was "very awkward for us," she told *J-14*, because they were constantly pitted against each other. "It was, 'Who's better at this?' and 'Who's better at that?' And then, the second season we kind of just had this tell-all talk where we started crying and really just put everything out there on the table, and that's when we became best friends."

MOVIE MOMENT: The second season of the show concluded with a ninety-minute TV movie, *Made in Japan*, which follows Rocky and CeCe to Tokyo to appear in a dance video game. Hijinks ensue, including getting fired from *Shake It Up Chicago* and a fight that ends their friendship—both of which are temporary, of course. Zendaya was especially excited about the TV movie because she and Thorne got to sing as well as dance, in the final sequence, when they perform "Made in Japan" for a cheering audience decked out in funky fashion. "I wear a classic Betsey Johnson dress," Zendaya told *Seventeen*. "It's edged up with a mini letterman jacket and some really cute Doc Martens that were actually custom-made for the movie. They have little black crystals on them and are so cute. I wish I got to keep them!"

REPEAT IT UP: All seventy-five episodes have "It Up" in the title. While some make sense like Season 1's "Give It Up" and "Add It Up," the show's writers had to get creative by the second and third seasons with "Three's a Crowd It Up," "My Fair Librarian It Up," and "My Bitter Sweet 16 It Up."

RATINGS SHAKE-UP: The pilot episode, "Start It Up," drew 6.2 million viewers, as the highest-rated premiere in Disney Channel history. Over its three seasons, *Shake It Up* did not slip in popularity as the No. 1 series for kids ages six to eleven and tweens ages nine to fourteen.

K.C. UNDERCOVER

ZENDAYA GOES SOLO WITH HER OWN SITCOM
PREMIERE DATE: JANUARY 18, 2015

High school math genius K.C. Cooper (Zendaya) balances life as a teenage girl and working as an undercover spy alongside her mother (Tammy Townsend) and father (Kadeem Hardison).

CREATOR: Corinne Marshall

CAST: Veronica Dunne, Kamil McFadden, Trinitee Stokes, Tammy Townsend, and Kadeem Hardison

NETWORK: Disney Channel

SEASONS: Three

NUMBER OF EPISODES: Seventy-five

OPENING THEME SONG: "Keep It Undercover" by Zendaya

AWARDS: Nickelodeon Kids' Choice Awards: Favorite Female TV Star (2016 and 2017)

GIRL POWER: The most significant thing Zendaya hoped to achieve with *K.C. Undercover* was female empowerment. "I wanted to make sure that there was a strong female character, and I think it's cool that young women and young men can both look up and say, 'Wow, I want to be like this girl,'" she told *Entertainment Weekly* in 2017, as the series came to an end after three seasons. "If you love something and you're excited, there should be nothing holding you back from doing that."

As mentioned earlier, one of her nonnegotiables for the show was that the teen spy may not be skilled at singing or dancing like *Shake It Up's* Rocky. "I want her to be martial arts–trained. I want her to be able to do everything that a guy can do. I want her to be just as smart as everybody else. I want her to be a brainiac. I want her to be able to think on her feet. But I also want her to be socially awkward, not a cool kid. I want her to be normal with an extraordinary life," Zendaya explained to *Teen Vogue*.

PRODUCING POWER: As the star and producer of the show, Zendaya was more involved in the storylines and development of the characters, beginning with her own: Remember Disney wanted to call the show *Super Awesome Katy*, but she changed her character's name to K.C., thus the name of the show?

One of the episodes of which she was especially proud was Season 3's "K.C. Under Construction," when the teen spy goes undercover as a construction worker—and is ridiculed by the men on the job site for being a girl. Sexism in the workplace may not seem like a natural topic on a kids show, but Zendaya felt it was important, and could be tackled in an age-appropriate manner. "There shouldn't be any labels on what type of path anybody should take or career simply because of their gender," Zendaya told *Access Hollywood*. "That makes no sense."

THORNE'S BACK: During the first season of the show, Zendaya's *Shake It Up* costar, Bella Thorne, made a special appearance as Jolie, a Russian spy who goes undercover as an exchange student—and then starts dating K.C.'s brother Ernie just to get information on the Cooper family. K.C. and Jolie settle it with a knockdown drag-out fight at school involving laser-shooting earrings, swords, parkour, and a watch that sprays sleeping gas. Rehearsing the scene was Thorne's favorite, she revealed to *Tiger Beat* in a joint interview with Zendaya, who playfully rolled her eyes and reenacted Thorne's over-exaggerated moves and sound effects. The best part about working together again two years after the end of *Shake It Up*, added Thorne, was "just getting to have our good old girl talks again."

MISTRESS OF DISGUISE: To play an undercover spy, naturally, Zendaya had to don a number of disguises. Among the most memorable: a punk rocker with spiky hair, a flight attendant, ballerina, circus performer, and biker babe. Some even required extensive prostheses, like the Season 2 episode, "Dance Like No One's Watching," in which K.C. goes undercover as a senior citizen named Bernie (one of four times she is disguised as a man) at a retirement home to track down a resident's grandson who is a smuggler.

CHILDHOOD IDOL: Growing up, Zendaya was a huge fan of Disney Channel's *That's So Raven*. Years later, on her own show, she got to share the screen with her childhood hero when Raven-Symoné made a guest appearance as Simone Deveraux, a former spy and computer genius. The two go undercover as janitors to rescue K.C.'s little sister Judy from the enemy known as The Other Side.

K.C. Undercover's executive producer Rob Lotterstein reached out to Raven-Symoné as a "gift" to Zendaya. Indeed, the experience was invaluable for the teen to work with the person who had taught her everything she knew about comedy. "It was kind of weird because I've learned so much from watching her, but I couldn't do her stuff in front of her," Zendaya confessed to *Variety*. "She really pushed me to try new things and create my own thing. I definitely had to step my game up."

SPECIAL GUESTS: Over the three seasons of the show, there were plenty of familiar faces in guest-starring roles, including Disney Channel favorites Skai Jackson, Peyton List, and China Anne McClain; *The Brady Bunch's* Florence Henderson; Jasmine Guy (Kadeem Hardison's costar on the 1990s sitcom *A Different World*); and Sherri Shepherd, who played recurring character Agent Beverly in seven episodes.

FINAL MISSION: *K.C. Undercover* ended on February 2, 2018. In the one-hour finale, "The Final Chapter," the teen spy must decide between going to college or becoming a spy full-time—and ultimately chooses both. While fans were sad to see the show go off the air after three seasons, Zendaya and her costar Veronica Dunne, who played K.C.'s best friend Marisa, saw the silver lining. "It comes to a great end," she told *EntertainmentTonight*, "and a beautiful family has grown up."

YOUNG AT HEART

Zendaya may have left Disney behind, but she still had a soft spot for creating children's programming. After starring in box-office smashes, such as *Spider-Man: Homecoming* and *The Greatest Showman*, she lent her voice to a pair of 2018 animated features: Netflix's *Duck Duck Goose*, as a duckling separated from her flock, and *Smallfoot*, a musical comedy with an all-star cast. Zendaya voices Meechee, a young yeti (an Abominable Snowman-type creature) and the love interest of Migo (Channing Tatum) who is searching for the mythical "smallfoot," a human being. Joining them on the hunt is Gwangi, played by LeBron James—Zendaya's costar in her next animated-live action flick, 2021's *Space Jam: A New Legacy*. The actress plays a modernized version of Lola Bunny, Bugs Bunny's girlfriend, who was scantily clad in the original 1996 film. In the sequel, the reworked character wears appropriate clothing for the young audience and is "feminine without being objectified," director Ryan Coogler told *Entertainment Weekly*. "For us, it was, let's ground her athletic prowess, her leadership skills, and make her as full a character as the others."

SPIDER-MAN: HOMECOMING

ENTERING THE MARVEL CINEMATIC UNIVERSE (MCU)
RELEASE DATE: JUNE 28, 2017

In the MCU superhero franchise, teenage Peter Parker (Tom Holland) must protect New York City from Vulture (Michael Keaton), while keeping his Spider-Man identity a secret from his friends, including MJ (Zendaya).

GENRE: Action/Sci-fi

DIRECTOR: Jon Watts

CAST: Tom Holland, Michael Keaton, Jon Favreau, Gwyneth Paltrow, Donald Glover, Tyne Daly, Marisa Tomei, and Robert Downey Jr.

RATED: PG-13

BOX OFFICE: $880.2 million

AWARDS: Teen Choice Awards: Choice Summer Movie Actress; Kids' Choice Awards: Favorite Movie Actress

---

MARVEL MYSTERY: When Zendaya auditioned at Marvel Studios in 2016, she had no idea for which character she was reading, although she did get the script ahead of time. The actress was not even supposed to know which superhero movie it was, "but I did find out that it was for *Spider-Man* 'cause I have good agents," she joked to *GQ*. "I just thought it was 'girl in *Spider-Man* movie.' I didn't really know what character, or what kind of character, they would be. Right before the screen test, they were kind of saying, 'okay, these are the characters that we're reading for, MJ being one of them,' and I was like 'oh that would be so cool!'"

SAME NAME: Zendaya's character is not the same MJ played by Kirsten Dunst in Sam Raimi's *Spider-Man* trilogy. Her initials are short for Michelle Jones-Watson, not the previous Mary Jane Watson—and also, Zendaya's MJ has a distinct personality. "My character is like very dry, awkward, intellectual, and because she's so smart, she just feels like she doesn't need to talk to people, like 'My brain is so far ahead of you that you're just not really on my level,'" she explained to *The Hollywood Reporter*. "So she comes off very weird. But, to me, she is very cool because she's deep. She's always thinking about something, always reading. I like that."

Also, unlike Dunst's MJ, Zendaya's character is not immediately a romantic interest for Peter (Holland), her Academic Decathlon teammate at school. So, then, why call her MJ? "She's not Mary Jane Watson, that's not who the character is," Marvel Studios' president and producer Kevin Feige explained to *Den of Geek*. "But giving her the initials that remind you of that dynamic certainly is intriguing about what could go forward."

NATURAL TALENT: As this version of MJ was unknown to Spider-Man fans, Zendaya was able to add her own flourishes to the character, suggesting that she wore no makeup. In fact, the actress went barefaced for her audition—and was totally unrecognizable to producers Amy Pascal and

Kevin Feige. "She was wearing no makeup and she was just dressed like a regular girl, and we were like, 'Oh my god, she's amazing. She has to be in the movie,'" Pascal recalled to *Vogue*. "And then we found out she was a totally famous person and felt really stupid."

ZENDAYA STAN: When the nineteen-year-old Disney star was cast in the film, the reaction was not overwhelmingly positive. For some critics, it was controversial for a Person of Color to play MJ. "Of course, there's going to be outrage over that because for some reason some people just aren't ready," Zendaya told *The Hollywood Reporter*. "I'm like, 'I don't know what America you live in, but, from what I see when I walk outside my streets of New York right now, I see lots of diversity and I see the real world and it's beautiful, and that's what should be reflected and that's what is reflected so you're just going to have to get over it.'"

One of the people who came to Zendaya's defense was none other than *Spider-Man* creator, Stan Lee. "If she is as good an actress as I hear she is, I think she'll be absolutely wonderful," the Marvel creative leader told the *Toronto Sun*. "The color of their skin doesn't matter, their religion doesn't matter, all that matters is that this is the right person for the role."

SPIDER-FAN: Zendaya admittedly was not a fan of *Spider-Man* as a kid, but she became "obsessed" with the superhero film franchise after seeing 2012's *The Amazing Spider-Man* starring Andrew Garfield—on her very first date, no less. "Spider-Man is always the coolest because he didn't come from money," she explained to *The Hollywood Reporter*. "He wasn't born with his superpower. It kind of just happens to him and he's just a kid, and he's just trying to balance living life and being a teenager and like hormones and problems and issues while also like doing the most outrageous things. He's always been the most relatable."

PASS THE TORCH: *Spider-Man: Homecoming* is the first *Spider-Man* film to join the MCU, following a 2015 deal between Marvel Studios and Sony to share the superhero's film rights. To welcome the young cast of up-and-comers were several familiar faces from the MCU: *Iron Man's* Tony Stark (Robert Downey Jr.), his fiancée Pepper Potts (Gwenyth Paltrow), and bodyguard Happy Hogan (Jon Favreau). In *Spider-Man: Homecoming*, Stark is a mentor for Peter, however much to Zendaya's dismay, she did not get to meet the veteran actor during filming.

For Downey Jr., being a part of the latest iteration of the superhero saga was "a blast," he said on *Good Morning America*. "I just love *Spider-Man* so to me being able to participate in reintroducing *Spider-Man* to a new generation or giving kind of a really back to, that's why it's called homecoming."

SUMMER BLOCKBUSTER: *Spider-Man: Homecoming* was the highest-grossing superhero flick of 2017—and the sixth-largest film based on an MCU character (at the time), behind *The Avengers*, *Avengers: Age of Ultron*, *Iron Man 3*, *Captain America: Civil War*, and *Spider-Man 3*.

THE GREATEST SHOWMAN

FLYING HIGH WITH ENSEMBLE CAST
RELEASE DATE: DECEMBER 20, 2017

The fictionalized story of P. T. Barnum (Hugh Jackman) traces the creation of his iconic circus and its stars, including beguiling acrobat Anne Wheeler (Zendaya).

GENRE: Musical/Thriller

DIRECTOR: Michael Gracey

CAST: Hugh Jackman, Zac Efron, Michelle Williams, and Rebecca Ferguson

RATED: PG

BOX OFFICE: $435 million

AWARDS: Kids' Choice Awards: Favorite Movie Actress; Teen Choice Awards: Choice Drama Movie Actress

---

FORBIDDEN LOVE: In *The Greatest Showman*, Anne's romantic interest is Phillip Carlyle, P. T. Barnum's business partner (Zac Efron). Portraying an interracial couple was special to Zendaya as "it was something that was not supposed to happen" back in nineteenth-century America and is unfortunately still not widely accepted two hundred years later. Anne and Phillip's relationship is a "constant battle of mind and heart," Zendaya said on NBC's *Today*. "The message within our characters is always allowing your heart to speak louder . . . I think this is a beautiful message about letting your heart speak and getting your happy ending."

REEL ROMANCE: Zendaya and Efron did not officially meet until *The Greatest Showman*, but they bonded instantly—and it translated onto the screen. Some fans were even convinced there might be something more there between the young actors. In addition to dating rumors floating around the internet, several videos on YouTube were edited to present the visual evidence: One five-minute clip titled "Zac Efron Can't Stop Flirting with Zendaya" racked up nearly ten million views, with thousands of comments discussing their chemistry.

The kiss between Anne and Phillip ranks as Efron's favorite ever, he revealed to Norway's FilmWebTV—which elicited a raised eyebrow from Zendaya. "Just because at this point for these characters, it's so built up, the tension between them is so strong, and literally, just a glance between them is electric. And, when they finally have the courage in that moment to finally connect and get that kiss, it's that epic musical moment."

HUGH BOOST: Once Zendaya was cast as Anne, first-time director Michael Gracey advised she start working on her upper-body strength to prepare for the on-set "trapeze rehearsal"—which was news to the actress. "I want to use the stunt double as little as possible," she recalled him saying on *The Tonight Show Starring Jimmy Fallon*. During rehearsals, she perfected her acrobatic moves from a rig that was a "comfortable" height and with the safety of a net. "And I show up on set, and yeah, the rig was like fifteen to twenty feet taller, and there was no net . . . because back in the day, they didn't have those yet." Hugh Jackman must have noticed Zendaya was a little anxious. As she prepared to climb into a cherry picker for the stunt's ascent, he walked by and marveled, "Zendaya, you're a badass"—and that was all the encouragement she needed. "I was like, 'Take me up!'"

SWING AND A MISS: One scene featured prominently in the trailer and promotion for the film is a trapeze sequence with Anne and Phillip— and it required a great number of takes to get just right. As they sing "Rewrite the Stars" midair, the two swing apart from each other before coming back together to spin in an embrace for the duet's climax. Zendaya and Efron learned the stunt's choreography on the ground, yet, once up in the air, gravity and momentum had a dizzying effect on the routine. "There are some very famous outtakes of them swinging in and just slamming [into each other] and just hanging limp," Gracey revealed to MTV. "It's not graceful at all!"

The tricky sequence was completed in one day, although the actors were originally told they would have a week. "We shot our hearts out," Efron recalled to BBC Radio 1. The footage was then submitted to the studio, who were so impressed with what the young actors had accomplished that they decided to allow Zendaya and Efron the full week to make it even better.

POPULAR SOUNDTRACK: Zendaya lent her voice to the musical, joining Tony Award-winning Hugh Jackman and *High School Musical* alum Zac Efron on several numbers, including "The Greatest Show," "Come Alive," and "Rewrite the Stars," a duet between Zendaya and Efron about their characters' predestined romance. All eleven performances in *The Greatest Showman* were recorded for the film's soundtrack, which sold over 5.3 million copies worldwide and earned a Grammy award. "Rewrite the Stars" was a moderate hit, peaking at No. 70 on the *Billboard* Hot 100 chart and winning Choice Music: Collaboration at the 2018 Teen Choice Awards.

ENCORE PERFORMANCE: A sequel to *The Greatest Showman* has been in development since at least 2019. "Those discussions have started, and we are working on one right now," Gracey told *The Sun*. Efron also hinted at a second installment during an appearance on the *Graham Norton Show*, revealing, "there is talk of something going around but no one is really sure." In recent years, Michelle Williams (who played P. T. Barnum's wife Charity) echoed fan sentiment that she hoped to continue the story with a sequel. Asked about her comments by *Variety*, in 2022, Hugh Jackman agreed they should, however, there was no concrete plan or script "that I know of yet . . ."

BOX OFFICE MAGIC: *The Greatest Showman* exceeded expectations, grossing nearly a half-billion dollars during its theatrical run, against a budget of $84 million—making it one of the most successful musicals of all time behind the likes of *Frozen*, *Mamma Mia!*, and *La La Land*.

STRIKE A POSE

Zendaya's influence as a style icon was confirmed by *Vogue* when the twenty-year-old landed the July 2017 cover of "the fashion bible," as labeled by the *New York Times*. Shot by legendary photographer Mario Testino, the pictorial illustrates the Disney star's glam transformation, as she dons Prada, Alexander McQueen, Dolce & Gabbana, and Calvin Klein in a mix of textures such as ostrich feathers, chain mail, sequins, and embroidered leather—"clothes that evoke just as much power and pizzazz as she does," raved the magazine. Zendaya could not wait to share the cover with fans, posting on Instagram to her millions of followers: "I really don't have any words right now. I'm grateful, honored, and a million other beautiful things that wouldn't fit in a caption. I'M ON *VOGUE*, Y'ALL!!!!" And it would not be the last time. The actress graced the cover twice more, as well as the British, Italian, and Australian versions. Looking back on her debut, "I felt very honored," she told the magazine in 2024. "I was just excited to be there, like, 'Put me in whatever you want.'"

EUPHORIA

ZENDAYA'S CAREER-DEFINING MOMENT
PREMIERE DATE: JUNE 16, 2019

In the town of East Highland, troubled teen Rue Bennet (Zendaya) and her high school friends navigate the complexities of life, love, loss, sex, and addiction.

CREATOR: Sam Levinson

CAST: Sydney Sweeney, Jacob Elordi, Angus Cloud, Hunter Schafer, Maude Apatow, Alexa Demie, Storm Reid, and Colman Domingo

NETWORK: HBO

SEASONS: Two (as of 2025)

NUMBER OF EPISODES: Thirty-six

OPENING THEME SONG: "Forever" by Labrinth

AWARDS: Primetime Emmy Awards: Lead Actress in a Drama Series (2020 and 2022); Golden Globe Awards: Best Actress

---

CHARACTER BUILDING: Although Rue (Zendaya) is the main character and narrator of the show, each episode focuses on the backstory of the supporting characters. In the first season, viewers got to know Nate Jacobs

(Jacob Elordi), a football star with anger issues, his cheerleader girlfriend Maddy Perez (Alexa Demie), her best friend, the sexually promiscuous Cassie Howard (Sydney Sweeney), and transgender Jules Vaughn (Hunter Schafer), Rue's on-off girlfriend. Season 2 concentrated on Rue's drug-dealing friend Fezco or Fez (Angus Cloud) and her childhood best friend Lexi Howard (Maude Apatow), who is also Cassie's younger sister.

TRIGGER WARNING: The role of Rue, a queer teen struggling with drug addiction, was unlike anyone the Disney star had played before—and she issued a warning to all her young fans ahead of the show's premiere. "*Euphoria* is for mature audiences," Zendaya wrote on Instagram. "It's a raw and honest portrait of addiction, anxiety, and the difficulties of navigating life today. There are scenes that are graphic, hard to watch, and can be triggering. Please only watch if you feel you can handle it. Do what's best for you. I will still love you and feel your support."

EMOTIONAL REALISM: Viewers may feel like they are experiencing their own state of euphoria watching the show, due to its highly cinematic lighting, camera movements, and editing intended to capture each character's inner perspective. The use of color also has special symbolism: saturated blues and purples reflect elation, while greens and yellows are for distress. The aesthetic reflects how teenagers imagine their lives to be, *Euphoria*'s director of photography, Marcel Rév, explained to *Deadline*. "We called it 'emotional realism' that's more based in the characters' emotions, and not how the world surrounding them really looks."

NOSTALGIC MIXTAPE: Music is a key component of *Euphoria*'s storytelling. Throughout the episodes—many of which are titled after popular tunes, like "Out of Touch" by Hall & Oates—the score is instrumental in adding depth to the drama. Levinson sought out English singer-songwriter Labrinth, who composed music inspired by the dynamics of the characters. "When I RIP" was written specifically for the scene in the pilot when Rue talks about her addiction.

Zendaya was such a fan, she recorded two gospel-inspired songs with Labrinth, "I'm Tired" for the Season 1 finale and "All for Us." Both were released on *Euphoria*'s soundtracks, which also feature popular music spanning all genres and decades, including Air Supply's "Even the Nights Are Better," INXS's "Never Tear Us Apart," Lenny Kravitz's "It Ain't Over 'til It's Over," and Tove Lo's "How Long."

BALANCING ACT: Zendaya took on the role of executive producer in Season 2, which allowed her to shape Rue's story behind the camera as well. In between filming the eight episodes, she was also busy promoting the 2021 blockbuster *Dune: Part One*, which forced her to jump between the troubled teen's dark world and her own world. The day she filmed the memorable scene in which Rue struggles to open a Jolly Rancher candy wrapper while experiencing drug withdrawal, Zendaya left for the prestigious Venice Film Festival. "I'm actually glad that I had this other thing happening in my life at the time, because it forced me to not psych myself out. I just landed, and I was like, 'I don't know what time zone I'm in, but we're going to jump right into it!'" Zendaya revealed to *The Hollywood Reporter*.

TRAGIC LOSS: Angus Cloud, an Oakland native like Zendaya, was working at a Brooklyn restaurant when he was scouted by the show's casting director to portray Fez, a kindhearted drug dealer. Despite no prior acting experience, he was so convincing as his character—because unfortunately he was dealing with addiction himself. On July 21, 2023, a week after attending his father's funeral, Cloud was found dead at his home. According to the coroner, the twenty-five-year-old accidentally overdosed on fentanyl, cocaine, and methamphetamine.

Zendaya urged fans to remember Cloud for who he truly was as a person. "I'm so grateful I got the chance to know him in this life, to call him a brother, to see his warm kind eyes and bright smile or hear his infectious cackle of a laugh," she captioned an Instagram tribute. "I know people use this expression often when talking about folks they love . . . 'they could light up any room they entered,' but boy, let me tell you, he was the best at it. I'd like to remember him that way."

SEASON 3: *Euphoria* was renewed for a third season in February 2022; however, production was pushed back a year due to Levinson's commitment to his other HBO show, *The Idol*—and then delayed even further by the 2023 Screen Actors Guild-American Federation of Television and Radio Artists strike. A year later, filming had still yet to begin, however, for Season 3, Zendaya hoped *Euphoria*'s storyline would skip ahead to the present day, allowing for the characters to no longer be teenagers. "I want to see what Rue looks like in her sobriety journey, how chaotic that might look," she told *The Hollywood Reporter*. "But also with all the characters, in the sense where they're trying to figure out what to do with their lives when high school is over and what kind of people they want to be ."

SPIDER-MAN: FAR FROM HOME

MJ AND PETER FINALLY MAKE IT OFFICIAL

RELEASE DATE: JULY 2, 2019

While on a European school trip with MJ (Zendaya) and Ned Leeds (Jacob Batalon), Peter is recruited by S.H.I.E.L.D. director Nick Fury (Samuel L. Jackson) and superhero Mysterio (Jake Gyllenhaal) to battle the villainous Elementals.

GENRE: Action/Adventure

DIRECTOR: Jon Watts

CAST: Tom Holland, Samuel L. Jackson, Cobie Smulders, Jon Favreau, J. B. Smoove, Jacob Batalon, Marisa Tomei, and Jake Gyllenhaal

RATED: PG-13

BOX OFFICE: $1.132 billion

AWARDS: People's Choice Awards: Female Movie Star of 2019; Teen Choice Awards: Choice Summer Movie Actress

CHARACTER GROWTH: MJ had a limited role in the *Spider-Man: Homecoming* movie, but the distinct character left an impression on audiences. In the sequel, Peter's love interest steps into a more prominent role as the teen superhero decides to confess his feelings during a school trip to Europe. It turns out that MJ feels the same, but her sarcastic personality prevents her from letting down the walls she has built up. "We get to see more sides of her character and how she responds in situations that make her a little more vulnerable and how her and Peter connect," the actress revealed to *Kidzworld*. "As this movie continues, through her awkward romance with Peter, she has to strip away her walls a little bit. She gets 'gooey' and you get to see this fragile young woman."

WORKING VACATION: The sights of Europe were not faked on a studio sound stage. *Spider-Man: Far From Home* was filmed far from the US: on locations in England, the Czech Republic, and Italy. Following along on the class trip overseas with Peter, MJ, and Ned, the audience also gets to check out famous landmarks such as the Tower of London, the Leonardo da Vinci Museum in Venice, and Prague's Carlo IV Hotel, which was built in 1890. In Venice, Zendaya shot a scene that called for her to stand in the Piazza San Marco covered in pigeons. "You know, that was not in the script," she joked on *Good Morning America*. "I got there and Jon [Watts] the director was like, 'Yeah, so we're gonna put some seeds on you and just let the pigeons go for it' . . . I was terrified, but I handled myself, I kept it composed. I've gotten over my fear of pigeons since then."

Most of the film's shooting took place in London, which is Holland's hometown, and he enjoyed showing Zendaya and Batalon around the city. When he was off filming scenes for the movie, the two went out exploring on their own, including a visit to the Harry Potter Studio. "So, while they were having so much fun, I was getting beaten up by a Hydro-Man," joked Holland, a Harry Potter superfan, to *Entertainment Tonight*.

STICKING TO THE SCRIPT: MJ is quite self-assured, and her deadpan sarcasm is what makes the character a fan-favorite. For Zendaya, that does not always come as naturally, so to match MJ's energy it was important that she memorize her lines verbatim. It was the opposite for her costars Holland and Batalon, who play best friends Peter and Ned, and therefore, often got to improvise their dialogue. "They can look at their lines once and go back and forth, have fun and make up lines because it works for the characters," Zendaya told *Kidzworld*. "Me, on the other hand, I can't. I would freak out and have a panic attack if I don't know my lines word-perfect. Also, MJ is so sure of everything she says that I can't. She never makes a mistake on anything really. She knows what she is going to say before she says it."

RED HOT: Zendaya sent fans into a frenzy when she showed up to the *Spider-Man: Far From Home* press event at the Tower of London with her hair dyed red—the same color as Peter's love interest, Mary Jane "MJ" Watson in the *Spider-Man* comic books. Zendaya fanned the flames when she posted her makeover on Instagram with the caption "Face it, Tiger . . ." For those who have not read the comics, MJ's most iconic line is the moment she first meets Peter in *The Amazing Spider-Man* #42: "Face it, Tiger . . . you just hit the jackpot." Zendaya confirmed the connection to *Entertainment Tonight*, admitting, "It was very intentional. It's a tribute to the OG character."

WILD RIDE: Just like most films in the MCU, *Spider-Man: Far From Home* features a mid-credits scene hinting at what is to come for the *Spider-Man* franchise. In it, Peter takes MJ, his new girlfriend, on a web-swinging tour of New York City—which ends up being so terrifying, she suggests they never do it again. The first time they shot the sequence, Zendaya and Holland were attached to wires and hoisted a hundred feet in the air to create the impression that they were really swinging between skyscrapers. However, "it didn't look as cool as we thought it was gonna look, even though we did drop a hundred feet," she revealed to *Entertainment Tonight*. In the re-shoot, "we ended up literally dangling a foot or two over the floor, with some fans," while director Jon Watts shook them.

DRESSED TO THRILL: Leave it to Zendaya, the style icon, to stun on the red carpet. At the LA premiere of *Spider-Man: Far From Home*, she paid homage to the film's new Spider-Man costume in a red-and-black color-block sequin gown by Armani Privé. "This is my own version," she explained to *Entertainment Tonight* when speaking about her *Spider-Man* inspired ensemble. Zendaya later revealed she was having second thoughts before stepping in front of the cameras. "I was just overthinking it a bit," she confessed to *Vogue* in 2024. "I was like, 'Do we have more options?' I was tripping. But it ended up being perfect."

SPIDEY CENTS: *Spider-Man: Far From Home* is the first Spider-Man film to ever pass the $1 billion dollar mark at the global box office. To date, it remains one of only nine MCU movies to reach ten figures, including 2021's *Spider-Man: No Way Home*. Only two films have surpassed $2 million: *Avengers: Infinity War* and *Avengers: Endgame*, both of which feature Holland as Spider-Man.

PARENTAL GUIDANCE

Every step of the way, Zendaya's mother and father have been right there, offering their daughter unconditional love and encouragement to achieve her every dream. People often asked the teen how she stayed so grounded, and she always credited her parents Claire and Kazembe— with whom she lived until she was twenty. That year, the couple split, but remained "homies," Zendaya tweeted the day of the announcement. Her individual relationships with each have flourished, as an adult. It was Zendaya who encouraged her newly single mother to cut her hair and get her first tattoo. "Look what I started," she joked as she pointed to her heavily-tattooed mother in a 2021 interview with Beyoncé's mother, Tina Knowles. Claire and Kazembe reunited in 2024 for the premiere of their daughter's film *Challengers*—and got an eyeful during its numerous sex scenes. "I thought it was hilarious," Zendaya told *Entertainment Tonight.* "It was funny 'cause, you know, obviously I've seen the movie many times, so I know what's coming, and they were all sitting behind me, and I got to watch them watch and slowly be like, 'Oh god.'"

DUNE: PART ONE

ZENDAYA'S SMALL ROLE MAKES A BIG IMPRESSION
RELEASE DATE: OCTOBER 22, 2021

The sci-fi saga follows Paul Atreides (Timothée Chalamet) as his noble family is thrust into a war over the desert planet Arrakis—as he's haunted by visions of a mysterious woman (Zendaya).

GENRE: Sci-fi/Adventure

DIRECTOR: Denis Villeneuve

CAST: Timothée Chalamet, Rebecca Ferguson, Oscar Isaac, John Brolin, Stellan Skarsgård, Dave Bautista, Javier Bardem, and Charlotte Rampling

RATED: PG-13

BOX OFFICE: $407.5 million

AWARDS: Nickelodeon Kids' Choice Awards: Favorite Movie Actress

---

HALF THE STORY: Based on Frank Herbert's 1965 novel, the *Dune* franchise is so epic, to truly do it justice, director Villeneuve decided to split it into two films. Warner Bros. agreed wholeheartedly; however, the studio would not give the green light to a sequel until the first proved itself at the box office. Once opening weekend exceeded all expectations,

Dune: Part Two was announced that Tuesday. The second film, originally set for a 2023 release, would pick up with Paul seeking revenge for the death of his father (Oscar Isaac) and restoring himself to power within the House Atreides.

DREAM GIRL: Zendaya plays Chani, a mysterious warrior who appears to Paul in his dreams, until they ultimately meet toward the end of the film. Although the *Euphoria* actress was featured prominently in promotion for *Dune: Part One*, fans were shocked to discover she was only in the film for seven minutes—4.5 percent of its total running time. Villeneuve assured Chani would evolve into a major character in the second part, although at the time, it had not been given the green light by Warner Bros, yet. "There's so much more to explore with these characters, with this world," Zendaya said on *Good Morning America* in October 2021. "I would love to be able to revisit these characters. I got a . . . small bit of time to hang out with everybody, and I would absolutely love to do it again because I feel like I learned so much, and it was one of the coolest experiences of my life. So hopefully people go see it and love it, and we'll be back."

TRUE BLUE: Chani's piercing eyes are an electric blue, the result of excessive use of a mind-bending drug called "spice." On the planet of Arrakis, it is the most significant commodity, therefore the vibrancy of her eyes is symbolic of her special powers—which Chani uses to communicate metaphysically with Paul.

BEST ACTRESS: Before casting even got underway for the *Dune* franchise, Zendaya already had her eye on the production. "I heard about it. And I was like, 'I really want to get in the room,'" she recalled to *Vogue*. "They weren't looking in my direction. And I was like, 'Hey, I'm here!'" The actress especially wanted to work with the Academy Award–nominated Villeneuve, best known for *Sicario* (2015), *Arrival* (2016), and *Blade Runner 2049* (2017). She made such an impression on the director during her audition, she effortlessly beat out the five other actresses all competing for the role.

"I remember meeting Chani for the very first time when Zendaya made me believe that she has been raised on an alien planet, in the deep desert, in the roughest environment," Villeneuve marveled to *Vogue*. "We all know Zendaya is a brilliant actress, but I was particularly amazed by the high precision of her acting skills, her intelligence, her graceful patience, and her great generosity. She's one of the most professional artists I've ever worked with."

FOREIGN LAND: Due to her limited role in the first film, Zendaya only spent five days on the set. By the time she was summoned to Wadi Rum, Jordan, to begin shooting her scenes, production was in full swing. "On my first day, I'm landing in what quite literally felt like Arrakis, because everybody was already in their costume when I met them. I was very intimidated," Zendaya recalled on *The Late Show with Stephen Colbert*. "Being there on that day, it was the coolest thing ever, but I was nervous." She didn't end up seeing any of the footage captured during filming until *Dune :Part One* was completed. "So when I got to see the movie, I was blown away," she told Stephen Colbert. "My jaw was on the floor in the same way, because I had no idea what other things [they] had shot. I just got to watch it as a fan."

DUNE DANCE: Despite Zendaya's short time on the set, she grew close with the cast, especially Chalamet, whom she regards as a lifelong friend. "I think my favorite part was when we would have these dance parties in my [hotel] room," she revealed on *The Late Show with Stephen Colbert*. "I would leave the door open and Timothée would come in with his little speaker, and everybody would come in and we'd start dancing." The cast member with the best moves? Javier Bardem, who plays Stilgar, leader of the Bremen tribe. "He was grooving . . . He had the moves."

DRAMATIC RELEASE: Much to Villeneuve's dismay, *Dune: Part One* was streamed on HBO Max simultaneously with its theatrical release the first month of release, as per Warner Bros.' post-COVID-19 hybrid distribution model. The director learned of the deal from the news, not Warner Bros., and he blasted the studio in an op-ed published by *Variety*. "There is absolutely no love for cinema, nor for the audience here. It is all about the survival of a telecom mammoth, one that is currently bearing an astronomical debt of more than $150 billion," wrote Villeneuve. "Streaming can produce great content, but not movies of *Dune's* scope and scale. Warner Bros.' decision means *Dune* won't have the chance to perform financially in order to be viable and piracy will ultimately triumph. Warner Bros. might just have killed the *Dune* franchise."

WORTH THE WAIT: This film—which was originally scheduled to be released in November 2020 but was delayed due to the COVID-19 pandemic—went on to gross $407 million at the global box office against a $165 million budget.

SPIDER-MAN: NO WAY HOME

ZENDAYA BLOSSOMS AS THE ROMANTIC LEAD
RELEASE DATE: DECEMBER 17, 2021

When MCU's multiverse breaks open, Peter gains two surprising allies. But, in order to save New York City, he must give up his two best friends, MJ and Ned.

GENRE: Action/Fantasy

DIRECTOR: Jon Watts

CAST: Tom Holland, Benedict Cumberbatch, Jacob Batalon, Jon Favreau, Jamie Foxx, Willem Dafoe, Alfred Molina, Marisa Tomei, Andrew Garfield, and Tobey Maguire

RATED: PG-13

BOX OFFICE: $1.922 billion

AWARDS: BET Awards: Best Actress; Nickelodeon Kids' Choice Awards: Favorite Movie Actress

---

MJ 3.0: Zendaya's character has come a long way since *Spider-Man: Homecoming*. With each film, MJ lowered her walls a little bit more—and, by the third movie in the trilogy, *Spider-Man: No Way Home*, she blossomed into a slightly less-sarcastic girl in love. "It's been really fun, especially [going] from the first movie being this really guarded, quiet, almost mysterious character that we know nothing about to watching the love story begin between her and Peter at the end of *Far From Home*," Zendaya recalled to *Screen Rant*. "And now, seeing how being with Peter has really opened her up. She's a very 'glass half empty,' negative person, but he brings out this hopeful, positive side of her. I think that's really sweet to watch—how they bring out these different parts of each other and rely on each other in different ways."

SPIDER-MEN: Past and present collide in *Spider-Man: No Way Home*, a crossover event featuring the actors who portrayed Peter Parker in previous *Spider-Man* films, Tobey Maguire and Andrew Garfield. Both play alternate versions of the character, "Peter-Two" and "Peter-Three," respectively, and shed some light on what they have been up to since we last saw them. For Peter-Three particularly, the return allows him to right a wrong from 2014's *The Amazing Spider-Man 2*, when he failed to save his girlfriend Gwen Stacy (Emma Stone) before she fell from a clock tower to her death. The tragedy was the catalyst for the end of his Spider-Man career—but, in *Spider-Man: No Way Home*, he gets a second chance.

During the climactic battle at the Statue of Liberty, MJ is knocked off the three-hundred-foot (91 m) monument. Peter-One rushes to save her but is intercepted midair by the Green Goblin (Dafoe), the same villain responsible for Gwen's death. Without hesitation, Peter-Three dives after free-falling MJ and catches her just in time. For Zendaya, working with Maguire and Garfield was a childhood dream come true. "I've always loved *Spider-Man*," she told *Screen Rant*.

BITTERSWEET ENDING: The conclusion of the trilogy was not exactly a happy one for Zendaya. Peter's decision to have Doctor Strange cast a spell that makes everyone forget he is Spider-Man ultimately saves the multiverse, but at the cost of his relationships with MJ and Ned (Batalon). "I cried throughout the whole movie. And the first thing I said when we finished was, 'This is awfully sad,'" Zendaya said in a joint interview with Holland for Marvel. "It's tough. It's bittersweet," he added. "It's very much just bitter," she quipped. "Like I'm not getting the sweet part." In the end, MJ and Ned head off to the prestigious Massachusetts Institute of Technology, and Zendaya wished Peter had joined them, instead of dropping out of high school (and unbeknownst to MJ, plotting Spider-Man's comeback). "It would have been so nice for them to go to college and just swing off into the sunset," agreed Holland. "Unfortunately, this is the way it is."

TALL TALE: Zendaya's three inches (7.5 cm) taller than Holland, which does not bother her one bit—although it did make their stunts a little trickier. In *Spider-Man: No Way Home*, there is a sequence where Spider-Man swings them onto a bridge and sets her down. The script called for it to be done "gently;" however, as the two were attached in a harness, the taller person would naturally land first—and that was Zendaya. "I'm the superhero. I'm supposed to look cool," Holland joked on *The Graham Norton Show*. He and Zendaya then recreated the scenario for the British TV audience. "I would sort of land like this and my feet would swing from underneath me," explained the actor as Zendaya wrapped one arm around his waist and the other held up his extended leg. "And she would catch me . . . It's so nice to be caught for a change."

HOME-WRECKER: After Holland accidentally revealed the title of the second film, *Spider-Man: Far From Home*, Marvel Studios decided to have some fun announcing *Spider-Man: No Way Home*. Zendaya, Holland, and Batalon each posted a different fake title on Instagram: *Home Slice*, *Phone Home*, and *Home-Wrecker*, respectively. In a follow-up video, Zendaya and Batalon are seen waiting outside the office of director Jon Watts. Holland walks out looking disappointed and informs them, "He gave us a fake name again. I just don't understand why he keeps doing this . . . Name me one thing that I've actually spoiled." Zendaya makes a face. "The last movie title." As the trio walk away, a whiteboard hanging on the wall spells it out for fans: *Spider-Man: No Way Home*.

BACK HOME: *Spider-Man: No Way Home* seemingly signaled the end of Marvel Studios' *Spider-Man* reboot, as it was the final film in the cast's contracts. However, the door was not closed—in fact, there was talk of a whole new trilogy starring the superhero and his friends. In February 2023, Feige revealed to *Entertainment Weekly*, "We have the story. We have big ideas for that, and our writers are just putting pen to paper now." However, the Writers Guild of America strike put all plans on hold for the time being. Seventeen months later, Feige finally had some good news to report. "We have writers who are going to be delivering us a draft relatively soon," he told *io9-Gizmodo*.

THIRD TIME'S THE CHARM: The third film in the *Spider-Man* series was ultimately the most successful—*Spider-Man: No Way Home* earned $800 million more than *Spider-Man: Far From Home* and $1.1 billion more than *Spider-Man: Homecoming*.

THE NEXT AALIYAH

The vibe of Zendaya's debut album reminded many people of another one-named double threat: Aaliyah, the R&B rising star who tragically died in a 2001 plane crash at the age of twenty-two. So, when Lifetime began production on a biopic about the late singer in 2014, Zendaya was the "one in a million" choice to cast. "She's been an inspiration and influence in my whole career, her talent still shines brighter [than] ever, all I wanna do is honor her," the Disney star wrote on Twitter (now known as X) as the news broke. Two weeks later, however, Zendaya dropped out of the project, citing a lack of production value, complications with the music rights, and, most importantly, that Aaliyah's family disapproved of the Lifetime production. "I just felt like it wasn't being handled delicately, considering the situation," she explained in an Instagram video. Another concern was that it felt "rushed," and, sure enough, five months later, *Aaliyah: The Princess of R&B* was released—and absolutely eviscerated by fans and critics alike. A decade later, it holds a 15 percent rating on Rotten Tomatoes.

DUNE: PART TWO
ZENDAYA EMERGES AS THE FRANCHISE'S LEADING LADY
RELEASE DATE: MARCH 1, 2024

Now united with Chani (Zendaya), Paul (Chalamet) immerses himself in Fremen culture on Arrakis, while plotting to seek revenge against those who destroyed his family.

GENRE: Sci-fi/Adventure

DIRECTOR: Denis Villeneuve

CAST: Timothée Chalamet, Rebecca Ferguson, Austin Butler, John Brolin, Florence Pugh, and Christopher Walken

RATED: PG-13

BOX OFFICE: $711.8 million

AWARDS: Nickelodeon Kid's Choice Awards: Favorite Movie Actress (nomination)

REAL DEAL: After her brief appearance in the first film, Chani became much more prominent in *Dune: Part Two*. Not only did the audience get to know the character better, but so did Zendaya. "She's not just in dreams this time," she promised the crowd at the 2023 *Dune* CinemaCon exhibit in Las Vegas (*Dune: Part Two* was delayed four months from its original

October release date due to Hollywood labor strikes). In an interview with the BBC, she admitted that in 2021's *Dune: Part One*, "I didn't really get to know [Chani]. Because we see her through Paul's visions and through his eyes. Now, we get to see her through her own eyes and who she is. And that's really exciting for me."

IT'S COMPLICATED: The love story between Chani and Paul is the epicenter of *Dune's* story, and the couple's dynamic is a fascinating aspect to what Villeneuve describes as "a war epic action movie." Chani is fighting to save her homeland from being colonized; however, Paul is part of the group that seeks to harvest Arrakis' supply of spice. "The universe of *Dune* is a complex world of geopolitics and with tons of ecological and technological metaphors that hold up today," Chalamet explained to *Vanity Fair*. "But, at the center, there's this relationship where Chani sort of becomes a moral compass."

Portraying the couple's honeymoon phase posed a challenge for Zendaya. "It was funny trying to figure out in this futuristic space talk, like, how do they flirt?" she mused to *Vanity Fair*. "What does that look like for a space warrior and the young duke of a planet? How do they show that they *like* each other? What does that even sound like? We were definitely trying to navigate that, which was funny because all of us were stumped. I think it's just as foreign to us as it probably is to the characters."

MAGICAL MOMENT: While filming the more romantic scenes in the Jordan desert, it was imperative to capture certain moments during "magic hour," the time just before the sun sets when its positioning casts a softer golden light. However, with only sixty minutes to get the scene right—or trek through the sand the next day and do it all over again—Zendaya and Chalamet felt the pressure. Nevertheless, they came up with a winning solution. "There's kind of, like, a ticking timer," she explained to *Vanity Fair*. "You kind of feel like, okay, we got here, but we have maybe an hour to get this. So, we revisited a bit every day, and over a few days, that gives us a few hours . . . . Every time we revisited it, we kind of got to sleep on it and think about it, and come up with a new set of ideas."

LIBERTIES: To prepare for her expanded role in *Dune: Part Two*, Zendaya studied up on Chani, listening to the audiobook "over and over again to see if there was anything that I missed, or things about her that I could hold onto," she told *Entertainment Weekly*. As a result, Villeneuve wrote the film character beyond the pages of the book, along with Lady Jessica (Rebecca Ferguson), Paul's mother. "In the second part of the book, Chani and Lady Jessica are a bit more in the background—which I didn't like, because I am absolutely in love with both characters," said Villeneuve. "I felt it was more meaningful to give them more substance and presence, their own agendas."

DESERT FASHION: As a warrior preparing to battle in the sands of Arrakis, Chani needed a little extra protection this time around. Costume designer Jacqueline West was inspired by medieval armor, yet with her own modern twist "to give that feeling of age-old, but now," she explained to *GQ*. Zendaya could attest to the medieval aspect. "When you first put it on . . . your shoulders hurt like everything's been squeezed in," she told the BBC. "Then, after a while you start to get some more mobility going." As they filmed in Jordan, the heavy costume trapped the heat in, she added, "so, that's not great. But it looks great, and that's all that matters."

MODERN MARKETING: TikTok was an important tool in marketing the *Dune* franchise, and the social team ramped it up for *Dune: Part Two*. Video content specifically featuring Zendaya and Chalamet were the most popular: The trailer that included their intros amassed seventy-six million views—compared to only seven million views without them. Meanwhile, traffic for the #Zendaya hashtag garnered over thirty-eight billion views. According to the movie marketing research company FanBox, all the extra promotion on TikTok (where the audience is primarily female) added another $2 million to the opening weekend's box office numbers.

PART 3: The *Dune* franchise did not end with *Dune: Part Two*—Villeneuve has written the script for a third installment based on *Dune Messiah*, the second novel in Frank Herbert's series. "*Dune Messiah* was written in reaction to the fact that people perceived Paul as a hero, which is not what he wanted to do," Villeneuve explained to *Empire* magazine. "My adaptation is closer to his idea that it's actually a warning." Hans Zimmer, who composed the scores of *Dune: Part One* and *Dune: Part Two*, also confirmed in 2024 that he was writing music for *Dune: Part Three*.

Would Zendaya be interested in reprising her role of Chani? "I mean, of course," she told Fandango. "Any time Denis calls it's a yes from me. I'm excited to see what happens. I started *Messiah* . . . It's so much to take in, but there's no better hands with better care and love for it than Denis."

GLOBAL HIT: *Dune: Part Two* grossed $712.4 million worldwide, with the majority coming from countries outside of North America. Overseas, the film exceeded expectations in its seventy-two foreign markets. Among the most popular were the United Kingdom, China, France, Germany, and Australia, all of which contributed more than $200 million to the total box office.

RECOVERING CHILD STAR

Fifteen years after realizing her dream of becoming a Disney kid, adult Zendaya started to wonder if it was truly worth it. In *Challengers*, she plays a tennis pro who spent her childhood perfecting her game, only for a career-ending injury to take it all away. The character's narrative gave her perspective on her own path to stardom, spending her teen years working nonstop and not going to school like a regular kid. "I don't know how much of a choice I had," she confessed to *Vogue*. "I have complicated feelings about kids and fame and being in the public eye, or being a child actor . . . And I think only now, as an adult, am I starting to go, 'Oh, okay, wait a minute: I've only ever done what I've known, and this is *all* I've known.' I'm almost going through my angsty teenager phase now, because I didn't really have the time to do it before. I felt like I was thrust into a very adult position: I was becoming the breadwinner of my family very early, and there was a lot of role-reversal happening."

CHALLENGERS

IT'S LOVE-ALL IN TENNIS-THEMED LOVE TRIANGLE
RELEASE DATE: APRIL 26, 2024

Former tennis prodigy, Tashi Duncan (Zendaya), is caught between her husband, Art Donaldson (Mike Faist), and her ex-boyfriend, Patrick Zweig (Josh O'Connor), who compete for her heart out on the court.

GENRE: Sport/Romance

DIRECTOR: Luca Guadagnino

CAST: Josh O'Connor and Mike Faist

RATED: R

BOX OFFICE: $78.7 million

AWARDS: TBD

LOVE ALL: The sports drama is centered around a love triangle involving Tashi, a retired tennis pro, her husband, Art, and ex-boyfriend, Patrick—allowing for the trio to equally share the screen. "What's special is that the three of us got to lead the movie," O'Connor revealed to the Associated Press. "An opportunity to do something like that is so rare." Their bond was just as strong off-screen, added Zendaya. "It's just the three of us. We are the cast. While we obviously have other amazing actors that contribute, this is the core thing here. Tennis training and the rehearsal period, it was just us. So thank god that we like each other."

OUT OF CHARACTER: Tashi is not the usual character that Zendaya has played thus far. "Typically, I play the person that ultimately is easier to empathize with," Zendaya told British *Vogue*. Tashi, however, is manipulative, pitting two lifelong friends against the other for her own pleasure. When Zendaya read the script, "There was something about her that felt very, 'Oh, damn.' Even I was kind of scared of her." However, she also sympathized with Tashi, who was forced to retire from her passion at a young age due to injury. "I'm grateful that I picked a career that I can keep doing for as long as I want to. I can be eighty years old and still be making movies if I get lucky enough to be able to or if that's something I still want to be doing then," Zendaya explained to the Associated Press. "I can't imagine that idea of that life or thing that makes you happy or gives you power being ripped away from you."

SHE ACED IT: As a producer on *Challengers*, Zendaya was involved in hiring the cast and crew. Her first was director Luca Guadagnino, best known for the 2017 coming-of-age drama *Call Me By Your Name*, which earned Chalamet an Oscar nomination. She's especially a fan of the atmosphere Luca Guadagnino creates in his films: "It's the looks, it's the glances, it's the tension," she told *Vogue*. "I feel he creates that visceral environment." For her costars and love interests, Zendaya also knew who she wanted: Faist, whom she had seen on Broadway in *Dear Evan Hansen*, and O'Connor from *The Crown*.

MÉNAGE À TROIS: Although there was one bedroom scene that had everyone talking, "tennis is the sex in the movie," Zendaya explained at the LA premiere. The sport "holds a metaphor for a lot of things—for desires, passion, pain, anger, frustration."

The buzzed-about threesome in *Challengers* was far less sexy to film, insisted the actors. "It is choreographed. It has to be so that everyone feels safe and comfortable," O'Connor told *People*. The sequence of Tashi, Art, and Patrick kissing had to be done in one shot. "So, that was like, 'Okay, you have to say this line, the camera's got to go here, and if we mess up, we got to start over again,'" added Zendaya. "It's very intentional and thought through with the help of everyone. It's such a community of people that make this one shot happen. It's like we [actors] are just a small part of it, ultimately."

GRAND SLAM: Finding the words to describe the movie *Challengers* is as complicated as its characters, Zendaya explained to *Sports Illustrated*. "I think it's not quite a tennis film. It's not quite a sports film, but it has tennis in it. I wouldn't say a romantic comedy, although there is romance and it's funny. I wouldn't say that it's entirely a drama, but there are dramatic moments. So, I think that's the beauty of it—it really can't be defined or categorized as any one thing. Just as I think the characters can't be defined or categorized. It's all just a complicated, beautiful mess."

TENNIS, ANYONE?: To accurately portray a tennis phenom, Zendaya spent three months training with Brad Gilbert, an Olympic bronze medalist who has coached Andre Agassi, Andy Roddick, and Coco Guaff. Five days a week, she would start her morning at 7 a.m. on the court for two hours of practice, followed by two hours in the gym. Initially, she struggled—until she looked at tennis the way she did dance. "Like, okay, it's more copying mannerisms, copying footwork, whatever. So, everything then became shadowing," she told *Vogue*. Instead of stressing about hitting the ball (which was later added digitally in post-production), she mimicked a body double's movements.

When she was not on the court practicing serves and swings, Gilbert took the actress to two collegiate matches. "One of 'em was over five hours, and Z didn't want to leave until it was over," he told *Women's Health*. "I think that really opened her eyes to seeing what a live match was all about." His wife Kim Gilbert also sent Zendaya videos of some of the greats, especially tennis pros who are tall like herself: Venus Williams, Maria Sharapova, and Naomi Osaka.

GAME, SET, MATCH: For the *Challengers* press tour, Zendaya stayed on theme. She wore electric lime—the color of a tennis ball—for the film's LA premiere. In the United Kingdom, Thom Brown designed a gown with embroidered tennis racket details. Loewe custom-made her white pumps with tennis ball heels for a photocall in Rome. Zendaya, who went blonde for the global trek, attended the Rolex Monte-Carlo Masters in a white pleated skirt and collared sleeveless shirt, inspired by 1957 Wimbledon champion Althea Gibson, one of the first Black professional tennis players.

PART THREE

Everything Zen

A TO ZENDAYA

As an actress, singer, dancer, and fashion icon, Zendaya has made such an impact on the world, it can be tricky to keep track of it all. Thus, whether you are an OG ZSwagger or new to the fandom, here is everything to know about the superstar, from A (Aunt Zendaya dotes on her many nieces and nephews) to Z (Zella, the nickname for Zendaya and Bella Thorne during their *Shake It Up* days). There are also the stories behind her very own Cinderella moment at the 2019 Met Gala; her Harry Potter obsession; her adorable dog, Noon; her Oakland, California, roots; and, of course, her longtime love, Tom Holland.

"I think it's kind of cool that my best friend in the whole wide world happens to be related to me."

AUNT ZENDAYA

Family is everything to Zendaya, and with five older siblings who have kids of their own, there is much love to go around for the Colemans. Zendaya has at least eight nieces and nephews who have popped up on her social media over the years, whether it has been family vacations, holidays, or babysitting adventures. She was actually born an aunt—her eldest brother Julien's daughter Zink is a year older—and the two have been lifelong best friends. "She's the yin to my yang," Zendaya told *Teen Vogue*, "the peanut butter to my jelly, the Nutella to my toast . . . . We have all the inside jokes you could ever imagine. We have all the memories for, like, four lifetimes. I think it's kind of cool that my best friend in the whole wide world happens to be related to me."

It is a different dynamic with the younger nieces and nephews. Aunt Zendaya helps with homework, paints their nails, carves pumpkins at

Halloween, and even picks them up from school on her days off. When she is working, she stays connected via FaceTime. The unique maternal role especially helped the actress portray a young mother in 2024's *Challengers*. "I have many, many little nieces and nephews. So, they're like my borrowed children," Zendaya told *People* magazine at the film's London premiere. "I get to have fun and then give them back to their parents."

BARBIE DOLL

Zendaya's iconic Oscars debut is immortalized as a one-of-a-kind Barbie doll. At the 2015 Barbie Rock 'N Royals event, the nineteen-year-old proudly unveiled her mini-me—and no detail was forgotten, "literally down to my pinkie ring," she marveled to *Teen Vogue*. Barbie Zendaya came with a replica of her Vivienne Westwood off-the-shoulder gown and clutch, diamond bracelet and earrings, and, of course, the famous hairstyle that *Fashion Police* host Giuliana Rancic said looked like it smelled of "patchouli oil or weed" (see page 134).

Zendaya loved the doll so much, she even made it her profile picture on Instagram. "When I was little I couldn't find a Barbie that looked like me, my . . . how times have changed," she captioned a photo comparison of the doll and herself. "Thank you @barbie for this honor and for allowing me to be a part [sic] of your diversification and expansion of the definition of beauty."

CINDERELLA MOMENT

A year after she had moved on from the Disney Channel, Zendaya paid homage to her past at the 2019 Met Gala. In keeping with the annual event's theme, "Camp: Notes on Fashion," she dressed as Disney princess

Cinderella in a steel-blue corseted Tommy Hilfiger ballgown with white puffy sleeves. Head to toe, every detail was perfected: blonde updo, headband, black choker necklace, Judith Lieber stagecoach clutch, and glass slippers—one of which Zendaya accidentally left behind on the Met Gala stairs like a scene straight out of the animated classic.

As photographers snapped away on the red carpet, her stylist Law Roach played the part of "fairy godmother"—with a flick of his magic wand (and some "Bibbidi-Bobbidi-Boo"), the dress illuminated in a mesmerizing shade of electric blue. The wearable technology was a three-month collaboration between Tommy Hilfiger and designer Hussein Chalayan, as a team of eight fitted the ballgown with twenty carbon fiber rods, five battery packs, and over a hundred feet of LED lights woven into the fabric. Once inside the Met Gala, Zendaya slipped into something a little more comfortable, yet still on theme—a pink dress like the one Cinderella's mice made for her to wear to the royal ball, until it was ripped apart by her wicked stepsisters.

Zendaya's evolution from *K.C. Undercover* to *Euphoria*, which would premiere three months after the Met Gala, is what inspired Law Roach to come up with the Cinderella concept. "It's almost like this is the last hoorah and the last time people will identify her as a Disney princess— which isn't a bad thing," he told *Vogue*. "Next year we're going to have to [either] chill out or come down from a helicopter like Diana Ross at the Superbowl. When this goes off like it's supposed to what else can you do!" As it turned out, COVID-19 and Zendaya's busy schedule kept her from returning to the Met Gala until 2024—when she shut down the red carpet in a custom Maison Margiela by John Galliano with a garden-themed gown festooned with metallic birds, berries, and vines.

DANCING WITH THE STARS

Long before acting, Zendaya's first passion was dancing (hip-hop and hula), and as *Shake It Up* came to an end in 2013, the sixteen-year-old competed on Season 16 of ABC's *Dancing with the Stars*. The Disney star and her partner Val Chmerkovskiy were early favorites, receiving the highest scores from the judges each week, including five "perfect tens" for their salsa, samba, hip-hop, freestyle, and instant jive performances. "When *Dancing with the Stars* is over, spread your wings, you're gonna fly away girl," judge Len Goodman praised Zendaya.

In the finale, a technical glitch made it difficult for fans to vote on ABC.com, and despite Zendaya and Chmerkovskiy being up by one point over Kellie Pickler and Derek Hough, she ultimately lost to the *American Idol* alum. Fans cried foul on social media, but Zendaya was a good sport and focused on the positives. "I'm very proud, and very happy, and I get to leave here with an amazing experience," she told cohost Brooke Burke-Charvet. Chmerkovskiy was equally complimentary of Zendaya—the youngest contestant ever on *Dancing with the Stars* up until that point. Her age (and the show's older demographic) made the teen initially skeptical about joining the show when producers first approached her. But, ultimately, she realized it was "good exposure," Zendaya revealed to radio host Mike Adam, "and I really wanted to learn. I wanted to try ballroom dancing out."

She did not win the coveted Mirrorball trophy, but Zendaya walked away with new fans. The loss remained Chmerkovskiy's "biggest heartbreak" on *Dancing with the Stars* he confessed to *Entertainment Tonight*. "She worked so hard, and I really wanted her to lift that trophy and jump-start her career . . . . But it jump-started her career anyway.

That's when you learn that it's not necessarily always about winning or losing, it's really about learning through the process and then using those tools to further yourself down the road."

EXERCISE ROUTINE

Sure, five-foot-ten Zendaya has been blessed by the genetic gods—but she does have to maintain her strength and stamina with moderate exercise. "I'm not the hugest fan of having to work out," she confessed to *Elle* in 2024. "I don't necessarily look forward to it." As a teen, the actress relied on choreographed dance routines to make exercise "fun." In her early twenties, she did high-intensity interval training (commonly known as HIIT) with a personal trainer, which included planks, pushups, crunches, squats, and lunges in between running laps around her pool in the backyard. During the pandemic, Zendaya found the motivation in quite an inventive way: "Because I missed acting so much, to inspire me to go downstairs and work out, I would wear different wigs. . . [and] come down in a different character," she revealed on *The Late Show With Stephen Colbert*.

To accurately portray a tennis pro in 2024's *Challengers*, Zendaya not only practiced her serves and backhands, but she also spent two hours a day working on agility and strength training with the goal to get "cut." Her full-body exercises consisted of overhead slams, curtsy lunges, Romanian deadlifts, chest presses, and squats with twenty-pound (9 kg) weights. To sculpt her shoulders, Zendaya's conditioning coach Bryan Doo added plate raises, cable presses, and moves with a TRX resistance band. Each workout ended with plenty of stretching and even a neck massage to alleviate any tightness. To fuel her body during these aggressive sessions, Zendaya upped her daily calorie intake and reached for protein bars and smoothies during rest periods. "She was up for anything that would make her look like a tennis player," Doo told *Women's Health*. "She really did anything an athlete would do."

FASHION ICON

After years of topping best-dressed lists, Zendaya received the ultimate distinction in 2021, when the Council of Fashion Designers of America (CFDA) named her the year's Fashion Icon. At twenty-five, she was the youngest to win the award—and accepted it in a custom look worthy of such an honor: a crimson Vera Wang silk faille bandeau and column skirt with an asymmetric hand-draped bubble waist from the creative mind of her stylist, Law Roach, who accessorized it all with sixty carats of Bulgari diamonds. "It's giving modern-day princess vibes if you ask me," he quipped to *Entertainment Tonight* on the red carpet beside his longtime muse.

The CFDA Fashion Icon Award was presented by Somali-born supermodel Iman, who praised Zendaya for exciting the world with her style and doing it so fearlessly for her young age: "Her instincts and confidence on the red carpet have redefined glamour for an entire new generation of fashion lovers, including my own daughter Lexi. She transcends any known definition of celebrity style we've become accustomed to . . . Zendaya reminds us all that true icons must always be brave and they will be forever ageless." The 2021 Fashion Icon recipient followed in the footsteps of Rihanna and Beyoncé. "Truly a dream come true for me," gushed Zendaya. "Fashion did something special for me. It gave me the extraordinary gift of transformation, the ability to become and embody all these difference characters and be literally anyone I wanted to be." After thanking Law Roach, her stylist since she was fourteen, Zendaya made a point to acknowledge "the smaller brands that dressed me before anybody else did."

GARDENIA

Zendaya's favorite flower is the gardenia, identified by its waxy white petals and a delicate scent described as slightly sweet with zesty undertones and a creaminess similar to coconut. She is such a fan, she has them growing in the backyard of her LA home. Inside, the gardenia scent is just as fragrant— Zendaya admitted on social media to buying ten gardenia candles so "every inch of my house smells like gardenia . . . my favorite scent in the world." While in Italy promoting *Challengers* in 2024, Fabio Fazio, the host of talk show *Che tempo che fa (What's the Weather Like)* presented a bouquet of gardenias to the actress, who seemed visibly moved by the sweet gesture. "These are my favorite flower," she gushed. "How did you know?"

HARRY POTTER

What does self-care look like to Zendaya? A *Harry Potter* marathon! "People say I'm crazy, but I watch *Harry Potter*, like once a day. It's just calming to me, so that's my thing," the lifelong superfan confessed to *InStyle* in 2019. "People are like, 'Oh my god, *Harry Potter* again?' I say, 'Don't come over to my house, if you don't want to watch it, because it's going to be on.'" The year before, Zendaya requested "something Harry Potter-related" to celebrate her twenty-second birthday with family in London, and that day the group visited The Making of Harry Potter studio tour at Warner Bros. The fangirl documented the excitement of the day on Instagram: a ride aboard the Hogwarts Express, a pint of Butterbeer, and "nerding out"

POP CULTURE EASTER EGG

As one of the rising stars of Generation Z, the fashionable actress often makes it a point to honor her style icons, sometimes in the most subtle of ways. At the London photo call for *Challengers* in April 2024, Zendaya made a statement in a Vivienne Westwood multicolored pastel striped vest and miniskirt—complete with a white feathered bustle resembling a bunny tail (illustrated on following page). Pop culture experts of a certain age immediately recognized the whimsical accessory made famous two decades earlier by television's most famous fashionista Carrie Bradshaw (Sarah Jessica Parker) on Season 4 of *Sex and the City*. Zendaya's archival two-piece first appeared on the Spring/Summer 1991 runway as part of Westwood's *Café Society* collection, albeit as a blazer. In keeping with the tennis film's sporty theme, her image architect, Law Roach had it transformed into a sleeveless vest for the modern style moment. To complete the look, Zendaya's new honey-blonde hair was swept up in a high ponytail with clip-in bangs, a fashion risk Carrie hasn't even tried yet.

over an intricately detailed model of Hogwarts castle used in the first film, 2001's *Harry Potter and the Sorcerer's Stone*.

Zendaya's favorite character is Harry Potter himself. "People may say this is basic," she explained to *GQ* in 2021, but not only is he the chosen one, "he's been through a lot and he's a G [gangsta]." Luckily for Zendaya, her boyfriend, Holland, is equally "obsessed" with the fantasy film series, and has also read all seven books. "I think I might know more about *Harry Potter* than [author] J. K. Rowling," he declared to BBC Radio 1 in 2020. Those words came back to haunt him in 2021 when the same interviewer gave Holland and Zendaya a pop quiz. The *Spider-Man: No Way Home* stars were three-for-three until the fourth and final question: What is the name of Neville Longbottom's pet toad? Holland knew the answer (Trevor), but Zendaya did not. "Good job!" she cheered. In 2022, the couple enjoyed a date night at the London stage production of *Harry Potter and the Cursed Child*—which Zendaya also saw on Broadway.

INSTAGRAM UNFOLLOW

Zendaya has scaled down her social media activity quite a bit in recent years, and at the start of 2024, she decided to wipe the slate clean altogether—she unfollowed everyone on Instagram, including her boyfriend Holland. This led to wild speculation that the couple had split, which the *Spider-Man* star insisted was "absolutely not" true, when TMZ caught him walking to his car in LA. For the record, Holland is still one of Zendaya's 184 million followers. Much to their chagrin, the only new content on her page is related to work, such as the *Challengers* trailer, the *Dune: Part Two* promotion, and her *Vogue* cover, as she chooses to keep her private life off social media.

Zendaya's not the first celeb to unfollow everyone—Billie Eilish, Olivia Rodrigo, and Timothée Chalamet also keep up with zero accounts on Instagram. The practice is not uncommon for people who want to stay off their phone more and find peace away from an increasingly toxic digital world. Zendaya has admitted to taking breaks from social media for her mental health. "I would find sometimes that being on it would kind of make me anxious, or I would start to overthink a little bit too much," she confessed to *People*. "[My fans] want me to be happy and exist beyond social media." And she advocates for others to do the same: "Take the time that you need and don't compare yourself to anyone else."

JOAN OF ARC

Zendaya's all-time favorite Met Gala look is one for the history books. For the 2018 event's theme, "Heavenly Bodies: Fashion and the Catholic Imagination," she dressed as patron saint Joan of Arc in a custom Versace chain mail gown designed to resemble armor with a studded metal collar, shoulder guards, and belt. "That dress was heavy as shit," she confessed to British *Vogue*. "Literally, I was sore the next day. It was like carrying a weight all night."

Once her stylist Law Roach learned the theme, he started brainstorming strong women who had a connection to religion. One night, he dreamt of Joan of Arc, a French teenager who fought in the Hundred Years' War—coincidentally, because she, too, had a vision. In 1428, Joan claimed the archangel Michael, Saint Margaret, and Saint Catherine all came to her and urged that she join the battle against English domination. Disguised as a man, she fought bravely as a military leader for two years until captured in 1430 by the British who accused her of acting upon

"Take the time that you need and don't compare yourself to anyone else."

demonic visions and wearing men's clothing. Joan of Arc, nineteen, was convicted of heresy and burned at the stake, and today remains a revered patron saint of France.

A short red wig made Zendaya's Joan of Arc transformation complete, and she "became this stoic warrior in every way," Law Roach told *Paper* magazine. "She has this way of stepping onto the carpet and becoming whoever the clothes call her to be . . . . It's incredible to watch."

KIZZMET JEWELRY

Zendaya's mother, Claire, turned her longtime passion for crystals into a business with her own jewelry line, Kizzmet, of handmade necklaces, bracelets, and earrings that radiate energy and healing powers. Each unique piece is tailored to the desires of its wearer, which is why Claire eschews listing products on her website. Instead, customers first take a brief personality quiz (favorite color, preferred chakra, and unresolved issues), and then she sends recommendations via email.

Of course, Zendaya's a big fan of her mother's "dope ass jewelry" and often wears Kizzmet creations, such as crystals like black tourmaline to ward off negativity, enhydro agate to symbolize emotional healing, and crystal quartz for harmony and stability.

Kizzmet—a play on *kismet*, another word for "destiny"—started as Claire making jewelry for herself from her collection of stones and crystals. As a result, her *kismet* was to start her very own line, and she already had a built-in clientele. "Friends and family asked nonstop for their own custom pieces," she wrote on kizzmetjewelry.com. "Letting your creativity shine can lead you to some amazing opportunities."

LAW ROACH

One of Zendaya's closest confidantes is someone who has boosted her confidence: her longtime stylist, Law Roach. The two first met in 2011, through a friend of Zendaya's father, when the Disney star needed help finding something to wear to the premiere of Justin Bieber's *Never Say Never*— and the rest is fashion history. As Zendaya's self-described "image architect," Law Roach was instrumental in her evolution from teen actress to one of Hollywood's best-dressed talents. "I don't think there's too many women in the world that does what she does on a red carpet," he confessed to E! News. "You could put a trash bag on her and she will not only look great, but she will feel great and she would sell that trash bag like it is a couture gown. It's just all confidence."

Before working with his "fashion soulmate," the Chicago native owned a vintage boutique in New York called Deliciously Vintage. After moving to LA and exclusively styling Zendaya, Law Roach's celeb roster boomed to include some of the biggest stars in entertainment: Celine Dion, Ariana Grande, Kerry Washington, Anya Taylor-Joy, and Megan Thee Stallion. Just like Zendaya ("my annoying little sister sometimes"), his clientele have become like second family. In 2022, Washington presented Law Roach with the first-ever CFDA Stylist Award, and in his acceptance speech, he thanked "all the women that have given me the opportunity and trusted me to dress them." Zendaya and Celine in particular "changed my life."

Law Roach announced his retirement in 2023, after an awkward moment at Paris Fashion Week went viral because it appeared he and Zendaya got in a tiff over a front-row seat at the Louis Vuitton show. That was not the case, and the false narrative on social media convinced the stylist to walk away from the industry—but not Zendaya, he clarified. "So, y'all really think I'm breaking up with Z, we are forever," Law Roach wrote on Instagram. "She's my little sister and it's real love, not the fake industry love."

MUSIC VIDEO CAMEOS

As a singer in her own right, Zendaya has starred in a dozen music videos, which have pulled in more than 600 million views on YouTube. This star power is why some of the biggest artists on the planet have tapped Zendaya for their visuals. In 2015, Taylor Swift invited the *Shake It Up* actress to join her all-star squad for "Bad Blood," as a knife-wielding assassin named Cut Throat alongside Selena Gomez (Arsyn), Gigi Hadid (Slay-Z), Ellie Goulding (Destructa X), Hayley Williams (The Crimson Curse), Cara Delevingne (Mother Chucker), and Karlie Kloss (Knockout). "There's a whole bunch of bad-butt girls running around it, it's awesome," Zendaya raved in a behind-the-scenes clip of the big-budget video, which has racked up more than 1.6 billion views.

"She's my little sister and it's real love, not the fake industry love."

Zendaya went from one superstar to another for her next music video cameo: Beyoncé's "All Night" from her 2016 album, *Lemonade*. The twenty-year-old was one of several rising stars cast, including Bey's protégés Chloe and Halle Bailey, Academy Award nominee Quvenzhané Wallis, and *The Hunger Games* actress Amandla Stenberg. When Zendaya got the call, she thought it was a prank—but, then, learned the real reason Beyoncé wanted her to be a part of it. "She said that she picked strong, powerful, inspirational women that she would want her daughter to look at," Zendaya told *Seventeen*. "I was just like, that's crazy. It was out of body."

The actress got a starring role in the music video for Bruno Mars' "Versace on the Floor" as his neighbor who gets so turned on by hearing him sing through the walls, she slips off her designer dress and walks next door to introduce herself. Zendaya caught Bruno's attention after impersonating him on *Lip Sync Battle*. "Apparently, he thought 'sexy girl in video' from that,'" she joked on *The Tonight Show Starring Jimmy Fallon*. Bruno clearly knew his audience—three million people watched "Versace on the Floor" in the first twenty-four hours of its 2017 release.

NOON

The lifelong animal lover grew up with a black giant schnauzer named Midnight, "one of the most loyal beings in my life." When he died in 2015, Zendaya was so devastated she could not imagine loving another pet again. But, on Christmas Day, her family surprised her with a gift that healed her broken heart: a miniature schnauzer puppy. "He's literally a mini Midnight"—so, she gave him a similar name, Noon. "What a beautiful gift . . . right when I needed it the most," she told fans in the pup's Instagram introduction. "I'm so thankful for this little man."

Noon lives the good life: He drinks Fiji water, travels via private jet, and is even carried around in Louis Vuitton purses. Zendaya takes him everywhere, from talk show appearances to Paris Fashion Week—but, at first, she could not even take him to a dog park. "He just loses it," she explained to "Dog Whisperer" Cesar Millan, who made a house call in 2017 to help train the hyper pup, as well as his owner. "Oh, I'm definitely an enabler," admitted Zendaya. "I'm definitely not good at telling him no." Luckily, Millan was able to break the bad habits and Noon went on to become BFFs with Holland's pit bull, Tessa, who sadly passed away in 2024.

Noon is so well-behaved, he knows not to bark when on set with Zendaya. "It is nice to go in your trailer after working long days and just having a little puppy there that just loves you and wants to see you every time," she told *GQ*. "Noon is absolutely my emotional support dog."

OAKLAND

Zendaya is a multigenerational native of Oakland in Northern California, a cultural melting pot with a rich history connected to the Civil Rights Movement. Growing up, she lived in the same house where her father was raised—the same place that hosted the Black Panther Party meetings in the basement in the 1960s. Although Zendaya has not lived in Oakland since 2009, she has maintained a deep connection to her hometown. She returns regularly to visit her extended family and donate her time to bettering the community that shaped her.

In 2023, Zendaya contributed to the renovation of several public basketball courts and was on hand for the big reveal. She even brought along a special guest, her boyfriend and *Spider-Man* star, Tom Holland, who showed off his hoop skills for the young fans in attendance. Zendaya has turned the British actor into a fan of her favorite NBA team, the Golden State Warriors, who play in nearby San Francisco. During the 2023 playoffs, the couple was spotted in the stands at the Chase Center cheering on the home team as they defeated the Los Angeles Lakers.

Zendaya also gave back to the organization that introduced her to acting. In 2024, the two-time Emmy Award winner donated $100,000 to the Cal Shakes Conservatory, which was so severely impacted by the pandemic, the theater did not produce any shows in 2023.

PERSONAL ASSISTANT

For the past decade, one person has been by Zendaya's side pretty much 24/7: her personal assistant, Darnell Appling. However, he is much more than that: "He's like a big brother, a mother, a grandmother, a chaperone, a guidance counselor all in one," she joked in a video created for the Zendaya

Growing up, she lived in the same house where her father was raised—the same place that hosted the Black Panther Party meetings in the basement in the 1960s.

app in 2017. Two years earlier, they had met on the set of *K.C. Undercover*, when Darnell was her stand-in due to their similar heights. The two hit it off immediately and he transitioned into the Disney star's assistant, and, ultimately, roommate as he handled everything from Zendaya's coffee orders to planning her first-ever vacation, when she was too stressed out about the thought of spending money.

Nevertheless, there has been plenty of perks to being her assistant: Darnell has traveled the world with Zendaya, escorted her to the 2021 Academy Awards, and in 2022, he landed a pivotal role in her film *Challengers* as the umpire of the titular match. The film's director Luca Guadagnino took notice of Darnell during a camera test, when he asked Zendaya if she needed anything. When he approached the assistant about the part, he agreed as long as his boss did too. "I looked over at Zendaya and she was like, 'Yes, yes, absolutely!'" Darnell recalled to *GQ*. So, is it

"I think we kind of created our own little look. It's kind of one of those things where either you love it or you hate it."

the start of his own acting career? "If it works out and it's in the stars, then I will do it, but I'm definitely not trying to quit my day job. I love my day job."

QUEEN OF THE MEME

Despite scaling back on her social media usage in recent years, Zendaya continues to go viral—most of the time inadvertently. The actress has been the subject of countless memes, whether it is her lol-worthy expressions or the rare fashion miss. "In every interview, I give them reaction pictures, meaning that I'll do a face, and they'll take that screenshot and use that for the rest of my life," she explained to Buzzfeed. In 2021, it was a split-second from the *Dune: Part One* press tour, as Chalamet is mid-flex and Zendaya just stares off into space. Mark Ruffalo even got in on the fun. The actor tweeted the screenshot on Twitter (now known as X), comparing them to his MCU character the Hulk. "Hulk" is typed out over Chalamet's head, while Zendaya is his scientist alter ego Bruce Banner.

Zendaya created her own viral moment when she posted a stunning photo of herself posing in a pool with the caption, "Out here living my best life." However, fans would not let her because Holland could be seen in the background floating. "Tom is drowning," replied a Twitter (now known as X) user. Zendaya eventually deleted the tweet altogether. She did not even have to do anything for "Zendaya Is Meechee" to go viral in 2018, when YouTuber Gabriel Gundacker recorded a song in which the lyrics are him reading the cast of *Smallfoot's* names on marketing posters. Within three days, the video hit nearly five million views.

One of her longest-running memes was born in 2014, at the *Teen Vogue* Young Hollywood party, when Zendaya accessorized her Emporio Armani jumpsuit with a giant hat by the Italian designer. "I put it on, and I was like, 'I'm like Erykah Badu meets Pharrell right now,'" the *Shake It Up* actress told *The Hollywood Reporter*. "I think we kind of created our own little look. It's kind of one of those things where either you love it or you hate it." The internet loved to hate it. In addition to the endless tweets, she inspired headlines like "9 Things That Could Be Hiding Under Zendaya's Giant Pharrell Williams Hat" and "Zendaya's Hat Is All We Can Think About." A decade later, "I stick by it," she declared to *Vogue*. "Me and Law, we thought it was chic at the time, I think it's still chic, I'd wear it again."

REAL ESTATE

Zendaya did not move out of her parents' home and into her own until she was twenty. In 2017, she purchased a $1.4 million Mediterranean-style residence with five bedrooms in the Northridge section of LA. Described in the real estate listing as an "entertainer's paradise," there were fourteen-foot (4 m) ceilings, LED ambiance lighting, designer porcelain flooring, a gourmet chef's kitchen, and a pool/spa in the backyard. Not long after moving in, Zendaya gave fans a glimpse inside of her home in a video tour for her now-defunct Zendaya app. "I'm from Oakland, humble beginnings. I have two parents as teachers, so I've never lived in a two-story house or a house with air-conditioning or a house with a pool, so this is crazy," she explained. "I have a staircase; it's like the Cinderella spiral staircase. I actually have one."

Two years later, she had much more with the purchase of a second property, a four-acre compound in Encino, about ten miles south in the San Fernando Valley. The ranch-style home has six bedrooms and seven bathrooms as well as private hiking trails, pool, and separate guest house. However, it does not seem Zendaya made the move—months later, she listed the investment property for rent. In April 2019, it hit the market for a cool $18,000 a month, but there were no takers until December, when the price was slashed to $14,900.

Zendaya's real estate portfolio expanded to the East Coast in 2021 with a $4.9 million condo in the brand-new Quay Tower, a thirty-story skyscraper on the water in New York's Brooklyn Heights. The building's luxurious amenities include a rooftop terrace, fitness room (with Pelotons and boxing classes), a music room, and a pet wash station. Zendaya's unit has a little something extra: its own elevator that opens right into the three-bedroom home with floor-to-ceiling windows, custom oak cabinetry, and high-end Gaggenau appliances in the kitchen. It is not likely she has whipped up any of her favorite Cup Noodles, here—according to *Architectural Digest*, the condo was rented for $16,000 a month.

SKINCARE SECRETS

Zendaya's skin is as flawless as her red-carpet style, and she lives by the adage that less is more. "Consistency is key," she advised fans during a *GQ* Q&A. "Sticking with products and keeping it simple . . . like cleanser, moisturizer." As an ambassador for Lancôme, she recommends the brand's UV Expert Defense 50+ Sunscreen Primer & Moisturizer, which contains SPF 50—after all, daily sunscreen is her No. 1 beauty tip. She also does not leave the house without Aquaphor Healing Ointment, the solution for literally any skincare need. Her third must-have: clear lip gloss. "[It] looks great on everyone, very versatile," Zendaya dished to *Elle* in 2024. "You can put it over a color or just by itself."

When she's not working, Zendaya prefers a bare face, just like her characters in *Euphoria* and *Spider-Man*. Also, any time she does wear makeup, she is her own glam squad! "I've had so many horror stories and I've had so many makeup artists in the past," she confessed to *Vogue*, "that I kind of took all the good things from each of them and learned how to do it myself." Taking it all off before she goes to bed is the best beauty tip she has ever received, and Zendaya has a simple yet effective (and inexpensive) process: She first cleanses with SheaMoisture African Black Soap Clarifying Facial Wipes, tones her skin with Thayers Facial Toner Rose Petal Witch Hazel, and slathers on The Body Shop's Vitamin E Overnight Serum-In-Oil, "which makes my skin look fresh and feel so soft by the morning," she revealed on the Zendaya app.

TOM HOLLAND

When Zendaya signed on to star in *Spider-Man: Homecoming*, little did she know her on-screen love interest would also become her real-life boyfriend. Rumors about Zendaya and Tom Holland ignited after the 2017 film, but the two denied being anything more than good friends for years—until summer 2021, when they were photographed kissing in LA. Months later, on the red carpet for the final *Spider-Man* installment, *Spider-Man: No Way Home*, "Tomdaya" were no longer hiding and packed on the public display of affection for the cameras.

Still, they remain private, despite the occasional effusive post on social media. Zendaya gave fans an intimate peek at their relationship in an Instagram post celebrating Holland's twenty-sixth birthday, in February 2022, with a black-and-white snapshot of him hugging her from behind with the caption, "Happiest of birthdays to the one who makes me the happiest <3." The proud boyfriend has celebrated Zendaya's many achievements—*Dune*, *Challengers*, the CFDA Fashion Icon Award—each with gushy captions and plenty of heart-eyes emojis.

In 2023, engagement rumors swirled after Zendaya's nail artist posted a video of her manicure, and eagle-eyed fans spotted a gold ring on her finger engraved with initials, although it was unclear whose exactly. Some people saw "TH" for Tom Holland, while others thought it read "ZH"—which hinted the couple had secretly married. Either way, do not expect them to make a public announcement any time soon. "Our relationship is something that we are incredibly protective of and we want to keep as sacred as possible," Holland revealed to *The Hollywood Reporter*. "We don't think that we owe it to anyone, it's our thing." When he did speak about it, he was all smiles. In an interview with Buzzfeed, the actor not only admitted Zendaya was his childhood crush, but, also, "I'm happy and in love."

"I'm happy and in love."

UNLIKELY HOBBY

To pass the long hours on the set of *Spider-Man: No Way Home*, Zendaya picked up quite an old-school hobby: knitting. The actress first attempted (and promptly gave up on) making a puppy-themed rug by hand, so she fell back on a skill she learned from her mother. "I loved it as a pastime," she revealed on *The Graham Norton Show*. "I love little tedious activities, things that can keep your brain occupied." She brought along her knitting needles and yarn everywhere she went. Holland recalled filming an intense fight scene, with blood dripping down his face as he battled a goblin, "and I'd turn around and you'd just be there knitting."

Zendaya's unlikely hobby was perfectly timed. *Spider-Man: No Way Home* filmed throughout the winter of 2020, so that holiday season everyone on the set received scarves—the only thing she can successfully knit. "I was like, 'What am I gonna get everybody for Christmas?'" she

FASHIONABLY LATE

In 2024, Zendaya made her fifth appearance at the Academy Awards—and she nearly missed the start of the ceremony. The *Dune* actress arrived on the red carpet with mere minutes to spare yet she proved to be worth the wait, decked out in a dazzling pink-and-silver asymmetrical gown by Armani Privé that oozed Old Hollywood glamour. The night also marked her second time as an Oscars presenter. In 2021, she handed out the statuettes for both Best Original Score (*Soul*) and Best Original Song ("Fight for You" from *Judas and the Black Messiah*, performed by H.E.R.). Three years later, she had the honor of announcing *Oppenheimer* as the winner of Best Cinematography. Could Zendaya's next Academy Awards appearance be as a nominee? Fans and film aficionados alike predicted she was a strong contender for 2025 Best Supporting Actress for her grand-slam performance as troubled former tennis ace Tashi Duncan in *Challengers*.

told Norton. "I'll just make them some scarves. That's what I'm doing all day." Zendaya's boyfriend loved his gift so much, he picked up the hobby himself. In 2022, a video went viral on TikTok that showed Holland knitting on a commercial flight to Budapest, where Zendaya was filming *Dune: Part Two*.

VEGETARIAN

At the tender age of eleven, Zendaya was in the car with her father when they passed a slaughterhouse—and he explained exactly what happened in there. "I thought it was awful, all those animals getting packed up in there waiting to be killed," she revealed on the Zendaya app in 2016. "I couldn't believe that's how I'd been getting my meat! It wasn't until I saw the documentary *Glass Walls* by PETA that I officially decided to become a vegetarian. It's so terrible, and my conscience is just too heavy."

Sticking to a vegetarian diet is not so hard for Zendaya, since she has never liked the taste of meat anyway (aside from her mother's turkey burgers). However, the animal lover also does not care for most vegetables—but with the right seasoning and dressings, she has plenty of food options. Zendaya is especially a fan of fast food and can find veggie options at all her favorites. At Chick-fil-A, she recommends the Spicy Southwest Salad, minus the chicken, and veggie spring rolls are her go-to at Panda Express. Zendaya's Chipotle order? "Make your own salad bowl of cilantro-lime white rice, black beans, romaine lettuce, guacamole, cheese, and tomato salsa." At the popular California hamburger chain In-N-Out, "I do a grilled cheese with grilled onions and extra spread. It tastes just as good as the burger. And the 'animal style' [Thousand Island spread and pickles] fries are unreal."

WEALTH

One of the richest actresses under thirty, Zendaya has built her approximate $22 million-dollar net worth on an impressive acting resume spanning TV and film. Back in her Disney days, she reportedly made $140,000 per season for her debut in *Shake It Up* and earned a substantial raise with her own series, *K.C. Undercover*, raking in $400,000 for each of the three seasons. The teen also starred in several made-for-TV movies for the channel, including *Frenemies* and *Zapped*, which brought in another estimated $750,000. For winning second place on *Dancing with the Stars*, Zendaya reportedly was paid $345,000 (including a $125,000 sign-on bonus).

Starring as MJ in the *Spider-Man* trilogy is when Zendaya really started making money—although it took until the third movie to see the financial fruits of her labor. According to reports, the actress received between $300,000 and $500,000 for the first two installments and $2 million for 2021's *Spider-Man: No Way Home*, plus another $10 million bonus from the $1.9 billion blockbuster. Similarly with *Dune: Part One*, Zendaya had a more significant role in the 2024 sequel, for which she reportedly earned $2 million.

As she reached her late twenties, Zendaya entered a new Hollywood echelon. For the third season of *Euphoria*, she negotiated a $1 million-per-episode salary, making the two-time Emmy winner one of the highest-paid actors in television. As a producer for 2024's *Challengers*, as well as the film's lead, Zendaya took home her biggest paycheck to date: $10 million.

X ZENDAYA

With millions of fans and a platform celebrating inclusivity and diversity, it is no surprise so many companies have looked to Zendaya to boost their brands. One of her first endorsements was Beats by Dre in 2012 when the fifteen-year-old Disney actress showed off her dance moves in an all-star campaign featuring Lil Wayne, Ellie Goulding, Zedd, will.i.am, and LeBron James. Since then, she's been the face of CoverGirl and Madonna's Material Girl clothing line, modeled for Valentino, Dolce & Gabbana, and Louis Vuitton, and promoted hydration as Glaceau Smartwater's global ambassador.

Since 2019, she has been a spokesperson for luxury cosmetics giant Lancôme, which sought out Zendaya for her "youthful and unique approach to beauty." The French brand has featured the superstar in ads for its Idôle fragrance, mascara, and most recently, foundation. "I like to look in the mirror and still feel like myself," she says in the 2024 commercial for Teint Idôle Ultra Wear. "I want my skin to still shine through."

Zendaya shuts down every red carpet she steps foot on, and, since 2020, every iconic fashion moment has been accessorized with Bulgari jewels. She has also starred in several print ads alongside fellow global ambassador Anne Hathaway, including the 2024 Eternally Reborn campaign celebrating the Rome-based brand's 140th anniversary. On her own, Zendaya is the face of Bulgari's B.zero1 line, described as innovative, daring, and "more than a jewel, a mindset."

YOUTUBE

Early in Zendaya's career, she gave fans an all-access glimpse of her life via YouTube, where she posted behind-the-scenes clips from *Shake It Up* and Hollywood events, as well as a cappella covers of some of her favorite songs, such as Michael Jackson's "Smile" and "White Christmas." Zendaya's very first video in November 2010 was shot at home with her friend's help

"I like to look in the mirror and still feel like myself."

and welcomed subscribers to her channel, "a place for happy, smiley faces and lots of love and dancing."

Seven years later, the actress rewatched it—and posted her reaction on YouTube. "This shit is so obnoxious," she joked, mocking her facial expressions and excessive cheeriness. "I was trying to make this positive environment and trying to be this ray of sunshine. . . . This was an act." Zendaya also relived her second video announcing her "official social networking sites," which also referenced "happy, smiley faces." Looking back at her fourteen-year-old self, she recalled thinking at the time, "I'm about to create this whole brand of positive smiling shit, Disney's gonna love this . . . . No wonder people were irritated with me. 'Oh, she is annoying.' Yes, honey, I was." Zendaya told her assistant, "I need to delete this," but, as of 2024, they are still up—and with a cumulative thirty million views and counting.

"She's always been amazing, and she's always going to be amazing."

There are several videos she took down from her official YouTube channel, which boasts four million subscribers. "Zendaya's Wavy-Curly Hair Tutorial," "Story Time: With My Mom," and "Inside My 20th Birthday" are among the titles no longer available to view. Much like her other social media platforms, Zendaya has been less active on her YouTube channel in recent years—her last video is a 2017 glimpse of the actress and Zac Efron filming the "Rewrite the Stars" scene from *The Greatest Showman*.

ZELLA

Zendaya was one-half of the Disney Channel's power duo known as Zella (or sometimes, Zendella) with Bella Thorne, her *Shake It Up* costar and partner in crime for three seasons. The teens were a packaged duo: They were side by side at fan events, recorded several chart-toppers like "This Is My Dance Floor," and shared the screen in the 2012 made-for-TV movie

Frenemies. Zendaya described their dynamic as similar to CeCe and Rocky's, "that perfect yin-and-yang thing," in her 2013 book *Between U and Me.* "What I love the most about Bella is that she's not afraid to be herself. She'll go up to someone and just say what's on her mind, and I respect that. . . . She has a lot of courage and guts, and she encourages me to let loose and take some risks when normally I wouldn't have."

However, the relationship was not always what it seemed, Thorne confessed in 2015, after *Shake It Up* went off the air. The first season "we wanted to love each other," she told *J-14*, but there was competition between the two starlets. Once they hashed it out, they became genuine BFFs who finished each other's sentences and hung out off the set—and that bond didn't end when the show did. When Thorne faced a nude photo scandal in 2019, Zendaya was there for her: "Just a reminder that you are strong and courageous and beautiful inside and out," Zendaya wrote in a text message according to *Elite Daily.* "You're a light and I'm super proud." The respect was mutual—Thorne has praised Zendaya's impressive post-Disney career and celebrated her first Emmy Award in 2020. "She's always been amazing, and she's always going to be amazing," Thorne told *Us Weekly.* "I'm just happy that people see that. That she's getting the recognition she deserves."

PART FOUR

Generation Z

VOICE OF REASON

Zendaya is not afraid to speak her mind. Since she was a teen role model, the actress has called out online trolls, body-shamers, racists, sexists, homophobes, and general haters. Over the years, her voice got louder the more she understood the importance of her words—and the power of social media (Zendaya has more than 180 million followers on Instagram). However, she would not consider herself an "activist," she explained to *InStyle*. "That is a lifestyle. That is a choice every day to be doing

> *"And it made me think,*
> *'How could I always have a lasting*
> *impact on what people saw and associated*
> *with People of Color?'"*

the work and devoting your life to a cause. And I don't feel I am deserving of the title . . . I'm an actress, but I'm also just a person who has a heart and wants to do the right thing."

SMELLS LIKE IGNORANCE

It was a major moment for Zendaya when she walked the red carpet at the 2015 Academy Awards, her first time ever attending the prestigious event. The eighteen-year-old was one of the best dressed, wearing an ivory off-the-shoulder Vivienne Westwood gown accessorized with a diamond cuff bracelet and earrings, and her hair twisted into faux locs. Unbeknownst to Zendaya at the time, E!'s *Fashion Police* host Giuliana Rancic was mocking her on the broadcast, joking that the hairstyle looks like it smells of "patchouli oil or weed."

In real time, viewers were shocked by the comment. The next morning, Zendaya expressed her own "awe" in a lengthy social media post. "There is a fine line between what is funny and disrespectful," she wrote of the "ignorant slurs" hurled at her by Rancic. "To say that an eighteen-year-old young woman with locs must smell of patchouli oil or 'weed' is not only a large stereotype, but outrageously offensive." The TV host apologized profusely, which Zendaya accepted. Looking back on the teachable moment years later, she felt it was important to speak up because "that's how change happens," she told *W Magazine* in 2021. "And it made me think, 'How could I always have a lasting impact on what people saw and associated with People of Color?'"

DAUGHTER DEAREST

Zendaya's parents, Claire and Kazembe, have always been her biggest supporters, and early in her career, it was not uncommon to see the two chaperoning their teen daughter at Hollywood events. However, in 2015, a Twitter (now known as X) troll decided to take a beautiful family photo and turn it into something unpleasant. "They made a gorgeous ass child lol," wrote the account, which has since been suspended. Another commenter added, "her parents really ugly I really would cry." The toxic tweets made their way to Zendaya, who did not hold back as she shut it all down. "First, I'm gonna pray for you," she began. "While you're so concerned about what my parents look like, please know that these are two of the most selfless people in the world. They have chosen to spend their entire life, not worried about trivial things such as looks and insulting people's parents on Twitter, but, instead, became educators who have dedicated their lives to teaching, cultivating, and filling young shallow mind[s]." Zendaya concluded her viral clapback by suggesting the troll not only "hug a teacher and read a textbook," but, more so, look within to see their own beauty "because such hateful things only stem from internal struggles. Bless you."

STARVING FOR ATTENTION

Did comedian Julie Klausner not learn anything from Giuliana Rancic? A year after the E! News host took heat for mocking Zendaya's hair at the Academy Awards, the *Difficult People* actress tweeted a "joke" about Zendaya's weight disguised as concern after watching her win Female TV Star at the 2016 Nickelodeon Kids' Choice Awards. In her acceptance speech, the Disney star especially thanked parents for "allowing me to be a role model for your children. I really, really do not take that for granted." Klausner, who did not attend the awards show, inexplicably put in her two cents mocking Zendaya as not a role model, but a "thinspo model for your impressionable tweens." In follow-up tweets, she doubled down: "Zendaya's ultimate retort to Giuliana Rancic is starving herself down to the size of one of her elbowz [sic]" as well as "You don't have to have an eating disorder to attend the Kids' Choice Awards . . . but it helps!"

Zendaya could not believe Klausner—twenty years her senior—would so blatantly body-shame her, and in a joking manner no less. "Do you find this funny?" she replied on Twitter (now known as X). "I will write another paragraph to educate you as well," she added, referencing the lengthy post she made to school Rancic. Fans also jumped to Zendaya's defense, but Klausner refused to back down. "I will never stop criticizing celebs who perpetuate dangerous beauty standards for a generation of girls who grow up thinking they're fat"—as if the five-foot-ten teenager could help her naturally slender frame.

DISTORTED REALITY

Zendaya traveled all the way to Puerto Vallarta to shoot the cover of *Modeliste*, in a picture-perfect tropical setting that was almost too good to be true. When the magazine hit newsstands in November 2015, Zendaya was shocked to see an image of herself pants-less in a black leather coat that had been digitally-manipulated to make her thighs and torso appear slimmer. She called out *Modeliste* on Instagram, posting a side by side of the real photo and the retouched version. "These are the things that make women self-conscious, that create the unrealistic ideals of beauty that we have," Zendaya wrote in the caption. "Anyone who knows who I am knows I stand for honest and pure self-love."

Modeliste immediately pulled the altered image from their site and released the full set of untouched photos—which unfortunately only further exposed the editors for being so heavy-handed in erasing Zendaya's baby hairs and even the jewelry they chose to accessorize her fashion shoot. "We are proud that Zendaya has taken this as an opportunity to address this situation, and create a very necessary honest and open dialogue," the magazine's editor-in-chief Amy McCabe wrote in an open letter. "I would also like to send a message to all of Zendaya's beautiful, shining, and loyal fans: We hear you and thank you for your outpouring support of the issue and this talented and inspiring young woman that we are all blessed to have as a role model and who will continue to inspire us through her artistic talents, intellect, creativity, and honesty."

A SEAT FOR EVERYONE

As a biracial woman, Zendaya has a unique position in Hollywood, one that she recognizes as a privilege compared to actors and actresses with darker skin. Because of this, she has made it a point to shine a light on colorism within

"That's the ultimate goal, to make room, [because] for a lot of Black creatives, it's not a lack of talent, but a lack of opportunity."

the industry—and use her seat at the table to make more room for others just as deserving. "I feel a responsibility to be a voice for the beautiful shades my people come in," Zendaya told *Cosmopolitan*, in 2016. Two years later, at the Beautycon Festival in New York, the *Spider-Man* actress opened up about being light-skinned. "I am Hollywood's, I guess you could say, acceptable version of a Black girl, and that has to change," insisted Zendaya. "We're vastly too beautiful and too interesting for me to just be the only representation of that."

To prove the color of an actor's skin should make no difference, Zendaya has told her agents to put her up for roles where the part "calls for a white girl," she revealed to *The Hollywood Reporter* in 2020. In fact, her *Euphoria* character Rue was based on the experiences of the show's creator Levinson, a white man. "So, Rue could have been that. [She] had no description," noted Zendaya. "I'm very grateful and, hopefully, . . . I can create things and make space for women who look like me and women who don't look like me. That's the ultimate goal, to make room, [because] for a lot of Black creatives, it's not a lack of talent, but a lack of opportunity."

SUSTAINABLE
FASHION

Zendaya is a classic beauty with timeless style, and she has singlehandedly revived vintage red-carpet fashion along with her "image architect" Law Roach who has mined the archives of Valentino, Versace, Cavalli, Mugler, and YSL. "People forget that vintage is sustainable; it's a way to reduce waste," he told British *Vogue* in 2020, the year Zendaya received the Visionary Award at the Green Carpet Fashion Awards. "And there's always a story: who's worn it before, who made it, what did it mean to them, where did you find it?"

"I want to reuse my clothes. I want to be able to wear that dress again when I'm forty and be like, "This old thing?""

The undisputed king and queen of archival dressing started pulling vintage pieces out of necessity early in her career, when high-end designers refused to loan clothes to Zendaya. "If you say no, it'll be a no forever," Law Roach recalled telling Dior, Gucci, and Chanel—three labels she has still never worn. At the time, the stylist had a vintage store in Chicago, and he relied on its inventory to dress his famous client. More than a decade later, they are building their own archive one fashion relic at a time, like a 2004 Louis Vuitton gold cropped blouse once modeled by Naomi Campbell and Givenchy's Fall 1999 motherboard dress that Zendaya wore to the *Dune: Part Two* premiere in Seoul. "We don't borrow from vintage dealers— we buy," Law Roach told *Vogue*. Zendaya sees it as an investment: "I want to reuse my clothes. I want to be able to wear that dress again when I'm forty and be like, 'This old thing?'"

MRS. ROBOTO

At the London premiere of *Dune: Part Two*, Zendaya channeled science fiction in an archival robot suit from Thierry Mugler's Fall 1995 couture collection. "Machinenmensch" (Machine Human) was inspired by Futura, a fictional robot from the 1925 dystopian novel *Metropolis*, and it took Mugler six months to create it with artist Jean-Jacques Urcun. Three decades later, Urcun lent his talents to Zendaya and Law Roach, helping dress her in the full metallic-and-plexiglass suit with built-in gloves the night of the premiere. "It was a dream to touch it, let alone get approval for her to wear it the way she wore it," Law Roach gushed to *Vogue*.

QUEEN Z

Recreating a Beyoncé moment is a risky move, but Zendaya pulled it off expertly at the 2021 BET Awards in the same Versace sheer purple halter dress worn by the "Crazy in Love" singer at the 2003 show. Zendaya's version had a slightly longer skirt, but the same accents of lime and violet. The Beyhive buzzed in approval, as did the designer herself. Donatella Versace praised the actress on Instagram with a series of photos of "sensational" Zendaya strutting in the couture creation. "I'll never forget Beyoncé wearing this in 2003," she wrote. "A tough act to follow but you aced it effortlessly!"

WORKING GIRL

At the 2021 Black Women in Hollywood Awards, Zendaya brought it all the way back to 1982 in a steel-blue satin puffed-sleeve top and slinky black skirt from Yves Saint Laurent. The ensemble, from Law Roach's personal archive, previously belonged to Black businesswoman Eunice W. Johnson, one of the founders of *Ebony* magazine—perfect for the event's theme: the resiliency of Black women in Hollywood through the years. Four decades earlier, the YSL look was featured in an advertisement celebrating the twenty-fifth anniversary of the Ebony Fashion Fair, which Johnson launched in 1958 as a hospital fundraiser and turned into an annual global tour highlighting African American fashion.

STAR IN STRIPES

Zendaya turned the *Euphoria* Season 2 premiere red carpet into a catwalk in a black-and-white vertically striped column gown with a scalloped neckline last modeled by Linda Evangelista at Valentino's Spring/Summer 1992 show. The actress—an ambassador for the Italian fashion house—made the look her own with minimal accessories: Bulgari Serpenti Viper diamond drop earrings and an eight-carat yellow diamond ring. Zendaya "perfectly embodies and represents what Valentino is and stands for, today," creative director Pierpaolo Piccioli said in a statement. "She is a powerful and fierce young woman that uses her talent and her work to express herself, her values, and her generation."

ONE MORE TIME

Zendaya has always wanted to raid Cher's closet—and she got the next best thing in 2022 when the singer's go-to designer Bob Mackie opened up his archive to Law Roach. For the TIME100 Gala, the stylist selected a teal and turquoise silk faille, emerald velvet strapless ball gown from Mackie's Fall 1998 collection, which he accessorized with a forty-nine-carat diamond Bulgari necklace. Zendaya's viral fashion moment "was a surprise of our career," Mackie's design director Joe McFate told *Vogue* in 2024. "She's a huge fan—and she looked so good in it."

DREAM ON

Off-duty Zendaya is the opposite of red-carpet Zendaya. She much prefers casual clothing, especially athleisure—and it inspired her partnership with On, a Swiss performance sportswear brand. In 2024, Zendaya signed a multiyear partnership with On and announced it with their first joint campaign, Dream Together, which focuses on how movement brings people together. As part of the rollout, the actress starred in a short film featuring hoodies, tights, and sneakers from the Zendaya Edit, modeled by herself and a group of interpretive dancers. "It's no secret that I've been a big fan of On for a long time," Zendaya said in a press release. "I'm always wearing them on set, or when I'm traveling, rehearsing, or running around with my dog. So it's a full-circle moment to make this partnership official." The *Dream Together with Zendaya* short film also reflects their shared values, she added: "I think this feeling of collaboration and inclusiveness shines through in what we've created."

THE POWER OF DIVERSITY

One of the most influential people in the world, Zendaya has used her platform to advocate for equality and inclusivity in fashion, beauty, Hollywood, and the world at large. "Obviously, representation and inclusivity are always something that I want to see," she explained to *Vogue*. "There's always work to be done. Sometimes there's not space given to you—you have to create it. There can't only be one of us, and sometimes you have to open the door and jam it open, so that others can come in, too. If there's not a seat there, go create your own table!"

FASHION FOR ALL

Inclusivity was the inspiration of her very own clothing line, Daya by Zendaya, a unisex collection of shirts, pants, jumpsuits, and jackets that embraced all body types with extended sizing (0–22). "I like playing with fashion and bending the 'rules,' or what was 'rules'—there are no rules anymore, you know? Fashion is way bigger than that and it's about wearing what you want and wearing what makes you feel comfortable and what makes you feel confident," Zendaya explained to *Elle* at the 2016 pop-up launch in New York City. "I do not believe in a label on a shirt or a dress should tell me that I can't wear a T-shirt or a pant because it should say women's or men's on it, you know?"

Fans agreed, as Daya by Zendaya flew off the virtual shelves online for over a year. In early 2018, she learned that some orders were not being fulfilled and customer complaints were falling on deaf ears, and immediately took matters into her own hands. Zendaya cut ties with the company she had hired to handle distribution, "but I will personally ensure that each and every outstanding order and issue is resolved," she promised in a statement. Looking back on Daya by Zendaya in an interview with *Vogue*, she admitted, "That was a big learning curve, for me. I was trying to figure out how to do all of it. Now, I'm just moving forward in different arenas of fashion. I've been learning."

FAMILY MATTERS

When Zendaya was offered her own sitcom, *K.C. Undercover*, only one thing mattered: "If I'm going to do this, this is how it has to be. There needs to be a Black family on the Disney Channel," she recalled telling execs in a 2017 *Glamour* profile. "A lot of people who aren't People of Color can't quite

"I do not believe in a label on a shirt or a dress should tell me that I can't wear a T-shirt or a pant because it should say women's or men's on it, you know?"

understand what it's like to grow up and not see yourself in mainstream media." Before K.C. Cooper's family of undercover spies debuted in 2015, Black representation on the network had been limited to *The Famous Jett Jackson* (1998–2001), *The Proud Family* (2001–2005), and *That's So Raven* (2003–2007). After *K.C. Undercover* came to an end in 2017, Raven-Symoné returned to Disney for the spinoff *Raven's Home*, which ran for six seasons— and spawned yet another Raven-Symoné series, *Alice in the Palace*, announced in 2024.

For Zendaya, her demand for diversity "was my first time realizing that I could have a little bit of power and request things that I wanted," she revealed to *The Hollywood Reporter* in 2021. Four years earlier, in a conversation with *Black-ish* actress Yara Shahidi for *Glamour*, Zendaya touched on the responsibility she sometimes feels as a biracial person in

Hollywood. "Can I honestly say I would be in the position I'm in if I weren't a lighter-skinned Black woman? No."

REPRESENTATION ON THE RUNWAY

Zendaya's bold fashion statements caught the attention of veteran designer Tommy Hilfiger, who tapped the superstar to create two collections for his iconic brand. So much more than clothes, the Zendaya x Tommy collaboration revolutionized the industry when it debuted at Paris Fashion Week in 2019: The runway featured only Black models, and of all ages, shades, and sizes. Among the veterans were Beverly Johnson, the first Black supermodel to cover *Vogue*, and Veronica Webb, the first Black supermodel to sign a major cosmetics deal with Revlon. Modern models included Winnie Harlow, who lives with vitiligo, a condition that causes patches of skin to lose pigmentation. "I feel like we are paying homage to these women who changed our legacy," Zendaya gushed to *The New York Times*. "This is a proud and happy celebration of female beauty in all its forms."

The second Zendaya x Tommy collection debuted during New York Fashion Week at the legendary Apollo Theater in Harlem. Drawing inspiration from the big-name artists who once graced its stage—Aretha Franklin, The Supremes, Ella Fitzgerald—Zendaya created 1970s-themed pieces, modeled by a diverse selection of beauties such as a six-months-pregnant Ashley Graham and Halima Aden, who wore a matching hijab head covering on the runway. "Size inclusivity was a huge point for me," Zendaya told *USA Today*. "I just wanted everyone to be represented."

RAISING THE STANDARD

A woman of her word, Zendaya will not voice support for any brand she does not feel aligns with her own principles. In the beauty realm particularly, she believes it is important to embrace individuality and buck trends. At the age of nineteen, she was tapped by CoverGirl as a brand ambassador because "we love her energy, confidence, and willingness to experiment and express herself with makeup," P&G executive vice president Esi Eggleston Bracey said in a statement. "I know that, together, we will do big things and help evolve the perception of beauty today." Zendaya especially gravitated towards CoverGirl for its newly adopted mission to "celebrate authenticity, diversity, and expressiveness, while eschewing unrealistic and idealized category standards."

Three years later, in 2019, she pivoted to competing beauty brand Lancôme, which has made charity the fabric of its business model. The company's Write Her Future initiative donated $100,000 to ProLiteracy, an adult education nonprofit, in honor of their new spokesperson, the daughter of teachers. However, what really resonated for Zendaya was Lancôme's history of diversity. "They've always had a wide range of foundation shades for women of all different skin tones," she told *People*. "It was really important to me to align myself with a brand that was already doing that."

REAL WOMEN

Zendaya has portrayed a range of characters, but none were truly "flawed" until Tashi Duncan, the protagonist of *Challengers*. Moreover, she hoped to play more of those kinds of women in future projects. "She doesn't have to be perfect. She doesn't have to be likable all the time. She doesn't have to be demure or passive," Zendaya mused to nonprofit organization The Female Lead. "I think it's important to have female characters that are messy and reflect what it is to be a human. Because if we only see one type of perfect woman or ideal of what these characters are supposed to represent then it doesn't feel honest and it doesn't feel true to the experience of many, many, many different kinds of women."

In previous films, the actress had made slight adjustments to her characters to give them more dimension. In *Spider-Man: No Way Home*, MJ and Peter finally become a couple—and Zendaya insisted the awkward girl not change to validate why the superhero saw something in her. "He likes her for all of her quirks and the weird things she's into, the things that her whole life have made her a little bit of a loner," Zendaya described to *Entertainment Weekly*. "I think he's a little bit of a loner too, and that's why they find that connection." It is a different kind of romance in *Dune: Part Two*, but a similar complexity. As a warrior Chani falls in love with Paul on the desert planet Arrakis, she seemed almost too competent, so Zendaya added a hint of humanity. "Does Chani get awkward?" she wondered. "Does she know what that feels like?" Thus, it was just as strange for Zendaya and Chalamet, who became close friends since the first *Dune*. "It's weird as hell," he joked to *Entertainment Tonight*. "I don't know what that says about the nature of our jobs, but it's just another day of work."

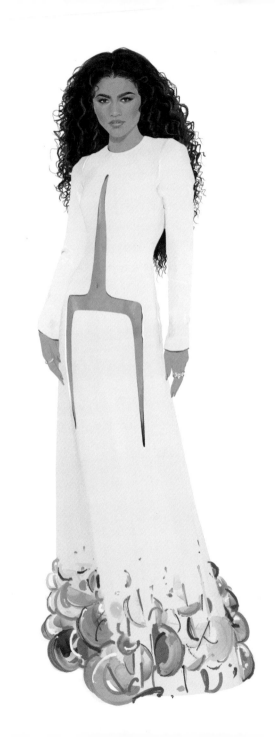

MODEL BEHAVIOR

With great power comes great responsibility, and Zendaya embraced that at the tender age of thirteen as the star of Disney's *Shake It Up*. Seemingly overnight, she was a role model to millions of young fans. Her character Rocky was someone to look up to: a sweet girl, good student, and dedicated friend. "*Shake It Up* definitely teaches kids about the importance of reaching for your dreams and setting high goals," Zendaya told the *Bay State Banner* in 2011. "It also teaches great lessons about friendship and family."

"You are the future leaders of the world. You are the future presidents, the future senators. You guys are the ones who are going to make this world better. You are the future."

Even as the show came to an end, she intended to remain a "positive influence," the sixteen-year-old actress told fans in a 2013 Disney video. "I'm very aware of the fact that I have young girls that watch me. They see what I do, what I wear, how I handle myself and it's important that they see someone closer to their age doing positive things and being involved in positive things . . . When it comes to what I wear and how I dress, they need to know you can still find confidence without having to show off too much."

Zendaya's self-awareness was in stark contrast to other former child stars struggling to find their identities in a post-Disney adult world. That same year, Miley Cyrus, who found fame as Hannah Montana for four seasons, embodied the title of her album *Can't Be Tamed*, when she shaved her head, stripped down to her underwear, and twerked on just about everything, including Robin Thicke at the MTV Video Music Awards, as millions around the world watched in concerned confusion. The paths taken by others was much darker. Demi Lovato had her first rehab stint at eighteen effectively ending her popular Disney series *Sonny with a Chance* in 2011; three years later, *Wizards of Waverly Place* star Selena Gomez also sought treatment for "substance abuse."

How could Zendaya avoid a similar fate? As she explained to *Complex*, she was more of a "real model"—a term she learned from rapper Tupac Shakur—rather than a role model. Disney graduates like Miley Cyrus "were forced into being role models and they had to pretend to be something that they didn't feel matched up with who they were. And that's because they started really, really young. So, you've got to realize when you're really young you don't know who you are yet. And as soon as you figure it out, you've already been forced to become something that you didn't really know you signed up for. So, it's like, I get it. There's a lot of pressure, so I completely understand. Everyone has their different ways of learning and growing and finding out who they are, and you can't fault people for that."

Zendaya's *Shake It Up* costar Bella Thorne echoed that sentiment. Three years after the show was canceled, she opened up about why she had always rejected the "role model" label as a young Disney star. "When you're trying to constantly do the right thing you end up making other people happy and not yourself," she told *InStyle* in 2016, three years before she began directing X-rated films for Pornhub. "I used to think 'Oh, I'm a role model, I need to look like this and do this and be this,' and I wasn't who I wanted to be."

On the contrary, this is exactly what Zendaya embraced. She carried over her principles to her own Disney series, *K.C. Undercover*, about a teenage math genius who moonlights as a spy. Three years running, she won Favorite Female TV Star at the Nickelodeon Kids' Choice Awards.

*"I have a heavy responsibility
on my shoulders."*

"To all the parents out there, thank you for allowing me to be a role model for your children," Zendaya said in her 2016 acceptance speech. The following year, as racial violence broke out in Charlottesville, she spoke directly to her young fans: "I need you to be educated. I need you to listen. I need you to pay attention. I need you to go ahead and understand that you have a voice, and it is okay to use it when you see something bad happen . . . You are the future leaders of the world. You are the future presidents, the future senators. You guys are the ones who are going to make this world better. You are the future. So, take that very, very seriously."

Even as she moved on from Disney, Zendaya held firm to her core beliefs—and her role as a "real model." In 2020, amid the Black Lives Matter movement, she joined protests and raised her voice to condemn racism in America. "I have a heavy responsibility on my shoulders," she told *The Hollywood Reporter*, "but I'm appreciative for that because with that there's a lot of good that I can do and I know who is watching."

ZENDAYA'S ROLE MODELS

The people who shaped Zendaya's life are an eclectic group ranging from pop culture icons to a seventeenth-century playwright. Her mother, Claire, is, of course, one of her greatest influences. A dedicated teacher for decades, she taught her daughter to embrace natural beauty by not wearing makeup. "I don't think she knew that to me, it was empowering that she didn't care," Zendaya told *Vanity Fair*. Her mother also introduced her to William Shakespeare, whose classics like *Twelfth Night* inspired her to get into acting as a kid. Modern-day role models include Michael Jackson ("the most talented person ever") and Beyoncé, who Zendaya met when she appeared in the singer's *Lemonade* visual for "All Night"—and was so starstruck, "I basically passed out," she joked on *Extra*. Zendaya was much more chill when she got the opportunity to thank another hero, Cher, whose iconic 1970s style on *The Sonny and Cher Show* encouraged her own fashion risks. "I've dissected and looked at a lot of the things that you've done that I think were pretty groundbreaking, especially for women," confessed Zendaya during a *Paper* magazine conversation. "So, I'm super inspired by you. I think [fashion] is just girl power in a sense."

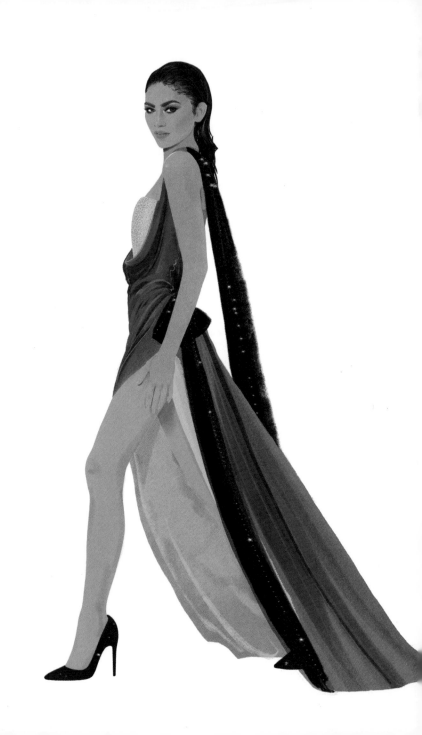

THE INTROVERT
REVOLUTION

J ust because she is outspoken, outgoing, and
the center of attention everywhere she goes
does not mean Zendaya is an extrovert. Quite the
contrary, "I'm a very shy, introverted person,"
she admitted in *Vogue*'s "73 Questions." Where
does she feel most at home? "At home" with her
dog. How does she unwind? "I just stay inside and
watch *Empire* and just, like, don't do anything."
Zendaya's introversion is not atypical—studies show
Generation Z (those born between 1996 and 2010)
have a higher percentage of introverts than any
other generation. The explanation, according to

Psychology Today, is that Generation Z is the first generation to have been raised with access to smartphones and social media, therefore, those technologies shaped their social lives.

Zendaya overcame debilitating shyness in her childhood; yet, "that shy kid" still exists within as an adult. However, now, she has the tools to cope. She has been open about going to therapy and regularly taking social media breaks for the betterment of her mental health. Early in her career, the young actress chronicled her life on Instagram and Twitter (now known as X), even though the oversharing often caused anxiety. As she began focusing more on self-preservation, she shared less. "I haven't been posting, and my fans probably hate it, which I understand," she told *People*. "But I get too overwhelmed with having to post things, and, if I think too much about it, I'm not gonna do it. It's not worth it."

As Zendaya became even more famous with *Spider-Man* and *Euphoria*, she became more recognizable. "There was a visceral change," she described to *Elle*. "Before, I could get away with going places and getting in and out." While filming *Challengers* in Boston in 2022, she skipped after-work outings with castmates O'Connor and Faist. "I would end up going right back home, because it was really overstimulating. Everybody would go hang out at a bar or something, and I'd be like, 'I'd love to, but I think I could ruin everybody's night. Because it's just not going to be fun once I'm there.'" Later that year, when she stepped out with boyfriend Holland to enjoy an afternoon at the Louvre in Paris, the famous couple became the main attraction. "You just kind of get used to the fact that, 'Oh, I'm also one of these art pieces you're going to take a picture of.' I just gotta be totally cool with it and just live my life," she mused to *Vogue*.

*"I'm a very shy,
introverted person."*

But it is not just the extra attention from fans—paparazzi also documented her every move, even if it was simply grocery shopping or taking her dog on a potty break. While in Italy in 2023, "I had this idea of, like, I can walk around Venice. No, I can't," she recalled with a laugh to *Elle*. "I had to pick up his poo, and I was like, 'Lord, please, don't take a picture of me picking up my dog's shit.' There's a picture of me holding the bag, but thankfully they spared the grabbing and the putting it in the bag part." This is why scaling back her presence on social media, and keeping precious moments private, has allowed Zendaya to regain some power. "I can't not be a person and live my life and love the person I love," she told the magazine. "But, also, I do have control over what I choose to share. It's about protecting the peace and letting things be your own but also not being afraid to exist. You can't hide. That's not fun, either. I am navigating it more than ever now."

"It's about protecting the peace and letting things be your own but also not being afraid to exist."

And one of the things she has learned is the power of "no." Zendaya built her career upon the unique bond with young fans, many of whom have grown up along with the actress. During her Disney days, she said "yes" to every single person who wanted to take a picture with the rising star "because you need to be grateful that you're here," she confessed to British *Vogue*. "And, while I still feel that way, I also have learned that I can say no, and I can say kindly that I'm having a day off, or I'm just trying to be to myself today, and I don't actually have to perform all the time."

Part of her healing journey has been exploring new hobbies. During the pandemic, Zendaya started painting at home, thanks to her friend and *Euphoria* costar Hunter Schafer, a talented artist. In an interview with *GQ*, she revealed a watercolor work in progress: "a naked, faceless woman who looks like she's on fire." She also revisited old passions, like music. At Coachella in 2023, she joined Labrinth for a surprise performance—

her first time onstage in a decade since touring behind her debut album, *Zendaya*.

Conquering her fear empowered her more than she could have imagined. Although she was only onstage for a few minutes, the love from the thousands of cheering fans reverberated endlessly. "My heart is so full," Zendaya wrote on Instagram. "I can't thank you enough for the love I received tonight, made all my nerves melt away."

As a kid, acting was one of the things that helped little Zendaya break out of her shell. All these years later, it is still the shy girl's secret weapon. Any time she is experiencing anxiety as an introvert on the red carpet or during an interview, she relies on what she knows. "Sometimes you have to psych yourself up and just pretend," she confessed on *The Kelly Clarkson Show* in 2024. "I'm an actor, so I pretend, and eventually you believe it."

A healthy dose of meditation, breathwork, and talking regularly to a therapist has helped Zendaya overcome mental hurdles, especially when she is not working and at home, where it is easy to self-isolate. "Sometimes it's just getting out of bed, telling myself, 'We're facing the day: we're taking a shower, we're putting on real clothes, we're seeing some sunshine,'" she explained to *Vogue*. "When I make myself do it, I realize it's actually kind of nice. I'm less anxious. I have to really be intentional about taking care of myself. I'm learning to be more responsible for myself and for my own body and looking after it all."

ACKNOWLEDGMENTS

Zendaya popped up on my radar back in 2013, the first time I heard "Replay"—a song that remains on repeat to this day. It was so fun to look back and retrace her steps from Disney to Hollywood, and every iconic fashion moment along the way. Thanks especially to the archives of Zendaya.com, ZendayaGallery.com, and @ZendayaStyleFiles on Instagram. I was able to organize fifteen years of TV appearances, print interviews, red carpets, magazine photoshoots, award shows, and more to write the ultimate Zendaya superfan guide.

ABOUT THE AUTHOR

Kathleen Perricone is a biographer with published titles about Marilyn Monroe, John F. Kennedy, Anne Frank, Barack Obama, Taylor Swift, Beyoncé, Harry Styles, and dozens more. Over the past two decades, Kathleen also worked as a celebrity news editor in New York City as well as for Yahoo!, Ryan Seacrest Productions, and for a reality TV family who shall remain nameless. She lives in Los Angeles.

First published in 2025 by Epic Ink, an imprint of The Quarto Group,
142 West 36th Street, 4th Floor, New York, NY 10018, USA
(212) 779-4972 www.Quarto.com

Epic Ink titles are also available at discount for retail, wholesale, promotional, and bulk purchase. For details, contact the Special Sales Manager by email at specialsales@quarto.com or by mail at The Quarto Group, Attn: Special Sales Manager, 100 Cummings Center Suite 265D, Beverly, MA 01915 USA.

10 9 8 7 6 5 4 3 2 1

ISBN: 978-0-7603-9500-4

Digital edition published in 2025
eISBN: 978-0-7603-9501-1

Library of Congress Control Number: 2024946141

Group Publisher: Rage Kindelsperger
Senior Acquiring Editor: Nicole James
Creative Director: Laura Drew
Managing Editor: Cara Donaldson
Editor: Keyla Pizarro-Hernández
Cover and Interior Design: Beth Middleworth

Printed in China